133 INT.   BASEMENT CLUB - ANGLE ON TABLE   NIGHT

ALAN and PENNY have each grabbed one of MIKE's arms
and are forcing him back into his seat.

                    MIKE
        I've got to go.

                    ALAN
        Wait till the number

                    MIKE
        I have no wish to wa:
        number's finished.

                    PENNY
        You can't be in that :
        hurry.

                    MIKE
        I can't stand this row
        girl ...
                (looks O.S.
                at stage)
        ... God, she's awful.

        Ssah!   VOICE (O.

MIKE desperately tries to whake
won't let go.

134 INT.   MESMER'S ROOM   NIGHT

MUSIC continues O.S. throughout.

The three are concentrating hard.
sags and whakes his head.

                    MESMER
        It's no use.
        be done

                                    30

61 EXT.   STREET OF CLUBS AND CAFES   NIGHT

ALAN, MIKE and PENNY strolling aimlessly, not
ease with one another.

                    PENNY
        Of course you could be the eccentric
        son of a duke. Bouts of amnesia.
        Split personality. Occasional fit:
        of lucidity -

                    ALAN
        Not that I've noticed.

They draw level with door of club in which
stands, hopefully looking out for custom.
stares at MIKE and recognises him. As h
slowly past she grows peeved.

                    RACHEL
        Hey, lover - remember me?

They all look back.   MIKE stares at he
insulting lack of recognition.

                    RACHEL
        Honest ... nothing to say to

                    MIKE
        Nothing you'd care to hear, m

                    RACHEL
        Gawd, I ask you! You had s
        pretty terrific things to sa
        night. And more besides.
        about actions speaking loude
        words ...

MIKE looks at her with disbelief an
moves on.   CAM TRACKS with the thi
at MIKE in disgust.

                    ALAN
        No wonder you prefer to e

                (To MIKE)
        Let's call it a day, sha

                    PENNY
        Is that what you'd call

110 INT.   BED-SI

MIKE and AUDREY are struggling madly on the bed.
MIKE is trying to strangle her.

        (N.B. - It would be worth shooting a lot
        of footage on this, taking it as
        far as it will go, but allowing
        for a dehydrated version for use
        in the U.K.)

                            from Sc.109,

                                        45

101 INT.   MESMER'S ROOM   NIGHT

CU TABLE. POKORNY's hand comes into frame and places
bottle on table. MIKE's hand moves in and picks
bottle up.

PULL BACK to take in MIKE, still tousled from the
ride. He puts bottle down, turns and goes out. We
stay on the door.

                    ESTELLE (O.S.)
        An' now ... tonight we try?

                    POKORNY (O.S.)
        The ultimate experience.

CAM PAN to take in MESMER from side angle. He spins
       to face us.

                    MESMER
        ultimate experience will be
        own deaths. I do not think

                                        40

97 Continued

                    PENNY
        Why?

                    MIKE
        Often the name isn't antique
        enough.

                    PENNY
                (getting up)
        I must go.

                    MIKE
                (idly, not getting
                up)
        What are you doing this weekend?

                    PENNY
        Oh, I've got an awful lot of
        things to do. I ... well, I ...

                    MIKE
        I'm taking Saturday afternoon of
        You come up as well - to hell
        with work - come with me.
        into the country.

                    PENNY
        Really, I ought to -

                    MIKE
        Ought! I OUGHT to be off down the
        Portobello road to see if I can
        pick up some old records of the
        Savoy Orpheans.

                    PENNY
        What for?

                    MIKE
        You can heat the records and take
        flower bowls out of them. The
        the really in' thing in
        U.S. I sell them by the score -
        or should I say by the gd?

                    PENNY
        But why the Savoy Orpheans specially?

                    MIKE
        They seem to melt more easily. (A
        BEAT) Saturday, then?

Shall we concentrate, then.

They move into a little huddle, their heads coming

THE SORCERERS

This first edition of *The Sorcerers*
is limited to 500 copies
of which this copy is

THE SORCERERS

THE ORIGINAL SCREENPLAY

JOHN BURKE

Edited by Johnny Mains

THE SORCERERS

All editorial work © Johnny Mains 2013

Foreword © Jean Burke 2013

Introduction © Matthew Sweet 2013

The Sorcerers Discord © Johnny Mains 2013

Treatment and Screenplay © Tigon Film Distributors 2013 and
both have been reproduced with permission

Letters are © Estate of John Burke 2013 and have been reproduced
with the Estate's permission

The Sorcerers Happening has been reprinted from *Michael Reeves* by
Benjamin Halligan and has been kindly reproduced with permission
from Manchester University Press. © Ben Halligan 2013

Liner notes from *The Sorcerers* DVD is © Kim Newman 2013

Michael Reeves: Britain's Lost Prodigy © Tony Earnshaw 2013

Interior Stills © Tigon Films 2013

Stills supplied by The Tony Earnshaw Collection

Photographs of John Burke © Jean Burke 2013

ISBN
978-1-848636-49-1

Design & Layout by Michael Smith
Printed and bound in England by T.J. International

PS Publishing
Grosvenor House | 1 New Road
Hornsea, HU18 1PG | England

e-mail: editor@pspublishing.co.uk | Internet: www.pspublishing.co.uk

Contents

Acknowledgements

Johnny Mains

T HIS HAS BEEN A LABOUR OF LOVE, BUT IT GOES WITHOUT saying, this book would have still remained in the blue boxfile marked THE SORCERERS without a fair few people sharing my vision for it.

To Pete and Nicky Crowther, who decided to do this book on the basis of one phonecall and a three minute get together at the 2012 Fantasycon. It's been a real thrill working on a book knowing that it's going to be brought out by PS Publishing, and I am truly over the moon that they have agreed to publish this quirky little bit of film history.

To John Henderson, who runs Tigon Film Distributors, and who has kindly given permission to let us reprint, in full, John's treatment and screenplay. Thanks also to Benjamin Halligan, who granted permission to let me reprint his chapter on the film from his excellent biography of Michael Reeves. It's a book that no cineaste should be without. Thanks also to Nicole Franklin at Odeon Entertainment and Marilyn Creswell at Manchester University Press for research and rights clearances.

Thanks also to Dr Matthew Sweet for his introduction to this book. He has been nothing but an enthusiastic and staunch supporter of this hair-brained scheme of mine to bring the screenplay to light ever since I first got in touch with him.

To Tony Earnshaw and the Tony Earnshaw Collection for supplying stills from the film and for his Reeves biography.

Additional thanks to Kim Newman for allowing me to reproduce his liner notes from the original DVD release, Christopher King, Nicholas Royle, Anne Billson, Stephen Jones, Mark Morris, Stephen Volk, Mark Gatiss, Pete Tombs, the folks at the *Behind the Couch* website, Martin

Roberts who sent me a copy of *The Sorcerers* when my copy went walk about—it's still to make an appearance—Mike Smith, for his excellent design work on the book—one of the reasons PS Publishing do the amazing books they do—and last but not least, my wife Lou.

Thanks most of all must go to two members of John's family; to Jean, his wife, and to Edmund (Ed), his son. Without their drive and support to see this project come to light, I don't think I would have thrown myself into this as quickly as I had without thinking about all the complications a project of this ilk brings if it hadn't been for their faith in me to do my very best in making sure that John's concept and work would not go unrecognised.

—Johnny Mains

Foreword

Jean Burke

MEMORIES ARE HAZY AND SADLY JOHN ISN'T HERE TO SHARE those times working on *The Sorcerers* with us, but I shall do my best to cast a little light on what was a very frustrating time for him.

We had watched the film together many times before he passed away, of course, and with each viewing the sense of injustice that he felt grew stronger. He pointed all the parts he had written, the bits that had been changed—and even though he said that kind of thing happened all the time back then, that it was the way of film business, he was undeniably hurt by the episode.

Once Johnny Mains had come into John's life, visited us, and saw John's original script for the film, he said that he would try to do something about it and try to right a wrong, but John thought that too much time had gone by and that nobody would really care.

John would be utterly thrilled by this book and the family would sincerely like to thank Johnny for the love and dedication he's put into bringing John's work back to life and to PS Publishing for thinking the project relevant enough to offer it to an audience who may be unfamiliar with *Terror For Kicks'* road to becoming *The Sorcerers*.

Extract From a Letter to
Raw Nerve Entertainment – October 1996

John Burke

WHAT I DO THINK SHOULD BE STRESSED IS THAT I DID NOT merely provide the "idea" for the screenplay. The entire original screenplay was my own, and it was on the basis of this complete script that Mike and Tony Tenser films set up the deal. At the last minute, Boris Karloff wanted some alterations to make him seem a more sympathetic and remorseful character, and Mike asked me to rewrite some concluding scenes to bring this out. I was very busy on another project at the time [Late Night Horror], and I said that I didn't really agree with Karloff's interpretation, but would forgo my final payment if he and Tom Baker would do the rewrites themselves . . . Tom Baker was, for a time, so far as I could judge, a flat-mate of Mike's who showed up for a couple of story discussions . . . They did so, and Mike assured me that as the main contributor I would still have top screenwriting credit. This promise was not honoured, but by the time I saw the finished product I was too busy elsewhere to make a fuss.

THE SORCERERS

The Sorcerers Discord

Johnny Mains

KIRKCUDBRIGHT, JANUARY 2011. MY WIFE AND I ARE STANDING in the office of John Burke, author of over 150 books—best known, perhaps, for his tie-in work, including *Hammer Horror Omnibus* volumes 1 and 2, *The Man Who Finally Died*, *Dad's Army*, *A Hard Day's Night* and *Dr Terror's House of Horrors*. While John is in his wheelchair, struggling with a blue and white cardboard boxfile (stubbornly not accepting any help), I am looking in wonder at the very first book I edited, which contains two stories by John. *Back From the Dead: The Legacy of the Pan Book of Horror Stories* is sandwiched between two collections, those of M.R. James and H.P. Lovecraft. It's a strange but very humbling feeling.

"You might be interested in seeing this," John says, placing the box on his desk. I turn around and look at what is written on the side in calligraphy pen.

THE SORCERERS

I open the box and pull out the screenplay—*Terror For Kicks*, John's original name for the film. I look through it, seeing where things had changed in Michael Reeves' finished film, as well as lines that I recognise. My hands are trembling. I pass the screenplay to my wife and delve deeper into the box, bringing out letters that John had written to Michael Reeves regarding the screenplay, contracts and the treatment for the film.

"Not only did I come up with the initial idea, I wrote the screenplay. Even the shooting screenplay that followed has my name on it," John says quietly.

I pull out the last thing in the folder, 120 loose A4 pages. On the top sheet:

"The Sorcerers"
Screenplay by
John Burke
Michael Reeves
&
Tom Baker

"And when the film came out," I say, "your name was dropped from the screenplay credits and you were relegated to 'from an idea by'? John, do you realise how *important* this all is?" John looks bemused but I know from our phone calls and letters that the whole *Sorcerers* issue still bugs him greatly. "Well, it was a long time ago," John says and we put the screenplay away and I place the blue boxfile back on John's shelf and we move onto the foreign editions of his books. I go all fanboy (again) when I discover a German tie-in edition of *Dr Terrors House of Horrors*.

On 20 September, 2011, John passes away. He has been beset by health problems for a couple of years but in the letters and emails I received from John in the last four or five months of his life, he seemed to think that time might be short. They had been distressing to read. One of his last letters to me concerned my second anthology, which I dedicated to him. He wrote that he thought the story by Reggie Oliver was "quite marvellous". Ten or so days after he dies I win an award for the book in which he has two stories. I dedicate the award to him with tears in my eyes.

In the months that follow John's death his son, Edmund, asks what I'd like of John's to help with putting together the unfinished autobiography he has on his computer. I ask if I could be sent the boxfile to *The Sorcerers*. I have a crazy notion that if I create a book about the original screenplay, or even publish the screenplay, then John might start to get the recognition he deserves for it.

A box arrives and I open it on the trunk in the lounge. It's a very weird, emotional moment. The last time I saw this file John was alive and I still want him alive. I miss him greatly. I bring out the blue boxfile, but I also bring out a red folder with *The Devil's Discord* written on it. Curiosity itches and I open up the folder, look at a screenplay (a haunted house film if there ever was one), a treatment then a few letters. "Holy shit!" I yelp. I leave the red folder on the trunk and run through to my office and pull open the top drawer to the filing cabinet. I start to go through all of the letters John wrote to me. I find what I'm looking for.

20th June 2009

". . . I had hoped to interest Chris [Christopher Lee] in a screenplay which I had written (The Devil's Discord), with a part in it angled at him and was bought for production by Raquel Welch's husband with an idea of featuring her also. Unfortunately they then split up—the sort of thing that kept happening in that world."

I take the letter through to the lounge, sit down and then pick up the letter from *The Devil's Discord* file. It is written by John and addressed to his agent Robin Dalton—the same Robin Dalton who would later go on to produce *Oscar and Lucinda*.

2nd December 1966

"You may remember that when you went away the Mike Reeves and Pat Curtis partnership had shelved Terror for Kicks *and were about to embark on* The Devil's Discord. *I went off to Broadstairs—and when I got back it was to learn that there had been casting trouble, [Forrest] Compton had backed out, and* The Devil's Discord *could not yet be made. But Boris Karloff would appear in* Terror for Kicks *if a rewrite was done to build up his part and alter the story somewhat. Mike Reeves wanted to know if I could drop everything and rewrite it to Karloff's wishes in a week or so.*

I had really had about enough of these folk, and after thinking over it I rang back and said I was too busy on another project (which is true) and couldn't do another week."

For a film fan, and for a fan of Michael Reeves, this news is quite staggering.

It's at this moment I want more than anything to pick up the phone and gibber down the line at John. Bend his ear some more. Instead, I put *The Devil's Discord* away and read my way through the boxfile for *The*

Sorcerers, at the same time I play the DVD. At the end of the film I resolve to make sure that the original screenplay for *The Sorcerers* is somehow published. As the weeks pass, I do lots of internet research and find that John Burke's name is hardly mentioned when it comes to the film. Even the official BFI website has John's involvement down to 'an idea by' when it is clearly not the case. I change the Wikipedia entry for *The Sorcerers*, thinking if people don't agree with it they can always change it back. To date, nobody has. It now says that the screenplay was written by John Burke, Michael Reeves and Tom Baker. I get in touch with Ben Halligan (biographer of Michael Reeves) and have a lengthy phone call with him one afternoon about his book, how he got in touch with John and if he thinks that bringing out the screenplay is a good idea. He agrees that it is.

Then everything is put on hold for many months. At the very end of November my wife tells me that we are expecting our first child. Not long after that, we get ready to move house and the *Sorcerers* files are packed up—but not forgotten about. They have a brief jaunt to London, where I show them to Matthew Sweet at the London Film Memorabilia event, but as July 2012 comes and Marnie is born four weeks early, these retreat to the back of my mind. At the end of September, I take the treatment, the screenplay to *The Sorcerers* plus a lovely related presspack to Fantasycon in Brighton. There was a phone call a little while before, where I talked to Pete Crowther from PS Publishing about the possibility of creating this book, but it's not until he sees what I've brought along that he agrees to do the book on the spot.

Not said to be one of Boris Karloff's best, but certainly a performance of stoic humility, *The Sorcerers* is certainly overshadowed by Reeves' last directorial offering, the classic *Witchfinder General*, but it is a forgotten classic and one that shows a seedy and distorted London not instantly recognisable to those who believe that flower power came into its own in 1966/67. The plot is a tried and tested premise; that of *The Sorcerer's Apprentice*. Boris Karloff plays Monserrat, a hypnotist who has been long discredited and is looking for a way to prove that he is not the charlatan the papers painted him out as. Monserrat has invented a device that can control minds and he and his long-suffering wife/assistant (an excellently deranged Catherine Lacey) are keen to try it out on someone who is clearly bored with life and is after vicarious thrills. That someone is the disaffected Mike Roscoe, (Ian Ogilvy) and they not only get into his mind, they can control him from afar, setting off a chain of events that results in a power struggle between Monserrat and his wife, with Mike their malleable pawn, now a killer, stuck in the middle.

This is not the first time that John Burke used the theme of a psychic couple — between 1976 - 1978 he would return to the concept with three novels (*The Devil's Footsteps, The Black Charade, Ladygrove*) concerning Dr Caspian and his wife, Bronwen. This time fighting for the side of good, they would use their powers to infiltrate people's minds and to some extent 'control' them if anyone was at peril. Their last outing, a short story called 'The Blackshore Dreamer' was published a year after Burke's death in *The Screaming Book of Horror* (Screaming Dreams, 2012). The DNA of *Terror For Kicks* used, this time, for good.

Other authors/directors have used the concept of people using their psychic abilities to enforce their will on others. An early example of this is George Du Maurier's 1894 novel *Trilby*, one of the most popular and feted novels of its time. *The Midwich Cuckoos* (1957) by John Wyndham, later filmed as *The Village of the Damned* (1960) and Stephen King's *Firestarter*, are probably the two most famous examples. The latter has certain people who can 'push' their wants and needs onto others and turn them into conduits. It was filmed (1984) to slight acclaim, with Drew Barrymore taking the lead role of Charlie McGee. One must also not forget *Scanners* (1981) which came out a year after *Firestarter* was published. Directed by David Cronenberg, this science fiction/horror crossover film certainly 'pushed' the concept of telekinesis and special effects to the limit.

It's mid-April as I sit in my office. If I look up at the bookcase on my right, the top two shelves are devoted to John's books. My desk is covered with letters in John's handwriting, his scripts for both films. I receive several emails from John's wife, Jean, and attached are lots of photos of John from around the time he wrote the scripts. I can almost hear him sighing at my sometimes questionable grammar.

You may be wondering why I care about bringing the original treatment and screenplay to *The Sorcerers* into print. I'm certainly not using this book to sully the legacy that Reeves left behind; it's that John, rightly believed that he hadn't fully put his side of the story across or proved his part—he did, to some small extent in Ben's book—but here for the first time is the proof that John Burke not only came up with the idea for *The Sorcerers*, but wrote the treatment for the film and the original screenplay. Because John declined to rewrite the end, Michael Reeves and Tom Baker took the credit for themselves. John Burke became a footnote and left the sorry mess rather battered and bruised. The treatment is the closest we will get to a novelisation of the film. Both documents should be regarded as historical documents, offering another perspective, the *original* perspective, on a strange little movie.

I am not going to talk about the differences between this script and the film, you can read Matthew Sweet's introduction and the chapter on *The Sorcerers* (reprinted here) from Benjamin Halligan's excellent biography of Michael Reeves, part of the *British Film Makers* series, first published by Manchester University Press in 2003. Ben does a better job of it than I ever could. Then what I'd like is for you to get your own copy of *The Sorcerers*—on video or DVD—put it on and compare the two.

In one of our phonecalls, John once said: "You have as much exhaustless enthusiasm as Michael had. He'd have liked you." All I can say is, John, look what you've made me do! I hope you like it, and if not, you can tell me off when we next meet.

An Account of a Different Season

Matthew Sweet

IN 1967, PHILIP LARKIN, POET, LIBRARIAN, CONNOISSEUR OF jazz records and jazz mags, reached two milestones in life—his forty-fifth birthday and his first fitting for a hearing aid. From his vantage points—a top-floor flat overlooking Pearson Park in Hull, his office at the University Library—he perceived a world populated by the unanxious young. Miniskirted students swished over the campus lawns: he remained inside, peering through the telescope he kept by his desk for the purpose of observing them. That year, two great poems were founded on this envy: *Annus Mirabilis*, in which, famously, Larkin dated the beginning of sexual intercourse to "between the end of the 'Chatterley' ban/ And the Beatles' first LP" and *High Windows*, in which the poet gazed, with jealous eyes, on "everyone young going down the long slide/ To happiness, endlessly."

1967 is remembered as the Summer of Love—at least by the 100,000 who converged on the San Francisco district of Haight-Ashbury to take LSD and think countercultural thoughts. ("A new concept of celebrations beneath the human underground must emerge, become conscious, and be shared," insisted the *San Francisco Oracle*.)[1] In Britain, too, some strove to achieve that state: at the London Free School in Notting Hill, at the UFO club on the Tottenham Court Road, at Alexandra Palace, where, on an unexpectedly rainy July night, the former home of the BBC became the site of the International Love-In. Pink Floyd played *Interstellar Overdrive*; a young crowd shared beer and pills and candy floss; everyone crashed out

---

1. *San Francisco Oracle* vol. 1 (1967), p. 2

on the floor. The surviving footage of the event captures the nervous, grinning faces of the audience: thin boys in thin jackets, long-haired girls
under white wide-brimmed hats. In British cinemas that year, their
fictional alter egos were projected on the screen: Barry Evans in *Here We
Go Round the Mulberry Bush*, attempting to mislay his virginity in the
pristine spaces of Stevenage; Rita Tushingham and Lynn Redgrave free-
wheeling through the Camden and Carnaby Street of *Smashing Time*,
turning a visit to a boutique or a greasy spoon into a Roundhouse
happening. The phrases that go with all this—Swinging London, the
Sexual Revolution, the Permissive Society—are as tenacious as they are
uninvestigated.

The Sorcerers sees 1967 through other eyes. They are those of Michael
Reeves, the bright young director who snuffed himself out before he
achieved full magnitude. But, as the contents of this book demonstrate,
Reeves's vision is a refinement and development of that of John Burke,
whose script, *Terror for Kicks*, is now revealed to be not a source for *The
Sorcerers*, but *The Sorcerers* itself. Its story of the disconsolate mod and the
mad scientist is not a vision of the summer of love. This is an account of a
different season. One in which the old, consumed with jealousy for the
freedoms of the young, use a kind of magic to gain vicarious experience of
those freedoms. One in which the young have discovered that the long
slide might lead to something other than happiness.

John Burke was two decades older than Michael Reeves. He was a man
of Philip Larkin's generation. (Only five months separate their birthdays.)
Burke was old enough to have served in the war; old enough to have
settled the terms of his life before literary men were expected to be full of
rage and dissatisfaction. His work as a Pan paperback writer gave him an
utterly unique viewpoint on the great cultural turns of the post-war period,
from the arrival of the Angry Young Man to the blossoming of Flower
Power. He took scripts by John Osborne and Ronald Harwood, images
composed by Richard Lester and Peter Watkins, performances by Tom
Courtenay and Oliver Reed, and processed them into prose fiction. It is
perfectly true and perfectly wrong to say that John Burke wrote *Look Back
in Anger*, *The Entertainer*, *Flame in the Streets*, *The Angry Silence*,
Smashing Time, *Privilege* and *A Hard Day's Night*. He was a Royal Court
writer who never had anything performed at the Royal Court; a man on
the crest of the British New Wave who was not invited to add his own
disturbances to the water. Surely the circuit formed by *Terror for Kicks*—

the envious old and the nihilistic young, thrumming with the same awful energy—must have been built with this material. "Oh to be young and vigorous," exclaims Estelle in *Terror for Kicks*, as deranged as she would be in the form of Catherine Lacey, "instead of taking our ecstasies second-hand . . . "

*T*error for Kicks was written two years before *The Sorcerers* materialised in British cinemas. That gap—as much as the generation one—explains some of the differences between the paper and the celluloid version of the drama. In Burke's script, the sensory vampirism of its older characters is achieved with a drug: a bottle of the sort from which Alice might have swigged. The guinea pig, Mike—"one of these children out on the street taking pills to keep themselves awake"—knocks it back and compares to it to Barley Water. Reeves's film rejects the bottle and barrages its version of Mike with imagery that is breathlessly contemporary: a *son et lumiere* of psychedelia, borrowed from the mind-bending work of Mark Boyle and Joan Hills, who filled Aldiss lamps with indigo ink and mealworms and drops of their own blood, and projected the results upon the walls of the UFO club and the Institute for Contemporary Arts. (A favourite Boyle family anecdote concerns the night that one of their light shows left Andy Warhol convinced that he was having an LSD-inspired breakdown.)

Another change between script and screen amplifies the sound of inter-generational conflict—though it's now harder to detect. In *Terror for Kicks*, Professor Marcus Mesmer, as yet only an image in the mind of John Burke, cruises the streets in his wheelchair. Burke imagines his encounter with Mike taking place on the pavement. In the film, Reeves brings the action to a Wimpy bar. Ian Ogilvy slouches up to the counter. "Give us a Wimpy," he says, with sullen primness—as Boris Karloff's Professor Montserrat prepares to woo him over the Formica. The environment now looks cutely archaic: the fortuitous capture of something that, in 2013, is heading off to join Hall's Distemper boards and Mazawattee tea in the Sargasso sea of cultural memory. In 1967, however, these wipe-clean surfaces suggested the future, not the past. Wimpy bars, reported *Time and Tide* magazine in 1961, were "the bright hope of the Sixties". For the heroine of Elizabeth Taylor's novel *The Wedding Group* (1968), the British burger joint represented a kind of heaven. "She dreamed of Wimpy Bars and a young man with a sports car, of cheap and fashionable clothes that would fall apart before she tired of them."[2] That fantasy now seems as old as Monserrat or Mesmer.

Youth and vigour are the qualities for which Michael Reeves is remembered. The struggle to experience their power is the idea at the heart of his film and the script from which it was conjured. A horror crowd in a cinema of 1967 would surely have felt the pull of those desires—particularly in those disreputable houses where staff would oblige older patrons by sitting them close to the more attractive members of the audience. But they also inform the biographies of those involved in the production. Behind the camera is the producer, Tony Tenser, the entrepreneur hoping to profit from Michael Reeves's youthful energy by locking him into a multi-picture deal. (In the early 1970s Tenser would leave the film business and settle down in Southport with a woman twenty-seven years his junior.) In front of the camera is Karloff, magisterially exhausted, the late-period star enjoying an infusion of young talent. There's also a teenage Susan George, who, after making *Straw Dogs* (1971), would form her own conclusions about what directors and audiences really think when they gaze on the image of a young actor. Most haunting, perhaps, is the figure of Victor Henry, the Royal Court hellraiser, star of the first revival of *Look Back in Anger*, full of bluff sincerity as Mike's best friend, Alan. In 1972 a hit-and-run incident propelled Henry into a coma from which he would never emerge. A 1976 article in the *Daily Express* depicted him lying in his hospital bed, glassy-eyed, a pair of headphones clamped over his ears; described how his mother, Margaret "a frail yet indomitable woman" would play him tapes of his old performances, in the hope that they might restore him to consciousness.[3] ("The pleasure of experiencing pain!" yearns Mike in *Terror for Kicks*. "The pleasure of experiencing anything!")

In the opening shot of *The Sorcerers*, Karloff's Montserrat looks dressed for a funeral, possibly his own. On some frowsty, littered street in an indeterminate stretch of west London, he passes a young couple as they bend towards each other for a kiss. He rolls his eyes in disgust. He walks on stiffly. (If you'd been there on the morning of the shoot, you may well have heard the squeak of the metal brace on the old actor's arthritic right leg.) For some, the film suggests, the summer of love came far too late. In *High Windows*, Larkin places this kind of jealousy in a historical context; imagines his own teenage freedoms as a source of envy to some middle-aged

2. *Time and Tide* 42 (September 1961), p.1259; Elizabeth Taylor, *The Wedding Group* (London: Viking, 1968), p.7.
3. Alan Bennett, 'Nobody is Going to Pull the Plug Out on My Son,' *Daily Express* (April 2 1976), p. 12.

observer, three decades back. It's now almost half a century since John Burke wrote *Terror for Kicks*. Anyone old enough to have seen *The Sorcerers* on its first run will now be nearer in age to Montserrat than to Mike. It is a film about the experience of growing old — an experience that few of us can escape. It became a cult picture not simply because it is minor, independent, and has been, for decades, the semi-secret pleasure of a cognoscenti. It is a cult because John Burke's script, like some new house built on a ley-line, it is alive with forces that it cannot quite marshal, and are timeless.

TERROR FOR KICKS

A film outline

by

John Burke

F.H.C. Productions Ltd.,
34, South Molton Street,
LONDON W.1.

of young Mods who go to the same
et up the town together, and knock
nny.   She is supposedly Mike's
lways made up a threesome: Mike
ne person at a time, especially
long.

ce in him and looks for kicks
ggressive: he can enjoy a
stretches without wanting
or to provoke trouble just
e, the tough, swaggering,
rampaging fits, Alan

Soho club where the
song.   Modern folk
, sometimes wryly
that is replacing
film we will in fact
llingly as we heard
essential part of the
today we don't have Greek choruses: we
throbbing, urgent music as a remorseless undertone
everything that happens before our eyes.   The whole film,
in fact, must be a with-it weirdie.

The Sorcerers Outline (Treatment)

TERROR FOR KICKS

A film outline
by John Burke

Copyright © 1965

F.H.C. Production Ltd.,
34, South Molton Street,
London
W. 1

Alan and Penny like folk song, but Mike is soon bored. He drags them out into the street with his usual feverish impatience but then is at a loss where to go. Where do you get the 'lift'? Strip clubs are deadly, the purple-heart crowd wandering about on the pavements are deadly ... tonight nothing is capable of giving Mike the kick he wants.

Alan and Penny are in favour of calling it a day and packing up. They argue loudly on a street corner and then leave Mike, who jeers after them. They grin at each other:

Mike turns impatiently away. An elderly man shuffles out of the shadows. He whispers that he can offer the young man a very unusual evening ... extraordinary experiences ... something very special. Mike is derisive. Blacked-out juice and a couple of faded blondes? Blue films? No, thank you - he's seen the lot.

Better than that, the old man assures him.

Drugs? Mike has tried them and they aren't worth the trouble. He doesn't intend to get hooked.

This will be worth the trouble, he is promised.

Because there is nothing else to do, Mike agrees to go along. But he'll beat up the old guy if he doesn't live up to his promise.

They go away from the garish lights down a dim side street to a decrepit old shop. Through the shop to a room behind -

gives the impression of being festooned with cobwebs ... aren't any actually there. Waiting are another ... stooped old woman with a face like a bird of ... looks round the room. A hell of a place for an

... creatures mutter among themselves. Is he ... he respond? Is he the right material?

... the old woman appreciatively. "So strong. ... uld be wonderful."

... Where's the action?

... is here now introduces himself as ... name means nothing? Ah, how soon fame ... his beautiful assistant Estelle ... 's greatest mind-reading teams at the ... Mesmer half bows to his beautiful ... rone.

... He didn't come here to watch ... ist act. And where does the ... "Is he the one you send round with

There is a threatening silence in the room. All three of them are sternly concentrating on him. Mike blinks. He feels dizzy.

Mesmer then solemnly assures him that there were no illusions in his act. Mesmer and Estelle were - and are - genuine telepaths, capable of reading other people's minds. All

Mike and Alan are a couple of a young Mods who go to
the same basement clubs together, beat up the town
together, and knock about with the same girl. Penny.
She is supposedly Mike's girl but somehow they have
always made up a threesome: Mike: Mike gets easily
bored with just one person at a time, especially a
girl, and likes having Alan along.

Mike has a streak of real violence in him and looks
for kicks the whole time. Alan is less aggressive: he
can enjoy a good basement club band for long
stretches without wanting to go restlessly on
somewhere else or to provoke trouble just for the
hell of it. But when Mike, the tough, swaggering,
dominating one, does have one of his rampaging fits,
Alan usually stands by him.

One evening the three of them are in a Soho club
where the music is entirely the latest fad - folk
song. Modern folk song. The bitter songs, sometimes
sad, sometimes wryly sentimental, sometimes harsh -
the music that is replacing beat, rhythm and blues.
Throughout the film we will in fact hear these songs
as insistently and compelling as we heard the zither
in The Third Man. It's an essential part of the
atmosphere, and at the same time a commentary on what
is going on in the story. Today we don't have Greek
choruses: we have this throbbing, urgent music as a
remorseless undertone to everything that happens
before our eyes. The whole film, in fact, must be a
with-it weirdie.

Alan and Penny like folk song, but Mike is soon
bored. He drags them out into the street with his
usual feverish impatience but then is at a loss where
to go. Where do you get the 'lift'? Strip clubs are
deadly, the purple-heart crowd wandering about on the
pavements are deadly, trad jazz in a basement is

deadly...tonight nothing is capable of giving Mike the kick he wants.

Alan and Penny are in favour of calling it a day and packing up. They argue loudly on a street corner and then leave Mike, who jeers after them. They grin at each other:

Mike turns impatiently away. An elderly man shuffles out of the shadows. He whispers that he can offer the young man a very unusual evening...extraordinary experiences...something very special. Mike is derisive. Blackcurrant juice and a couple of faded blondes? Blue films? No, thank you - he's seen the lot.

Better than that, the old man coaxes him.

Drugs? Mike has tried them and they aren't worth the trouble. He doesn't intend to get hooked.

This will be worth the trouble, he is promised.

Because there is nothing else to do, Mike agrees to go along. But he'll beat up the old guy if he doesn't live up to his promise.

They go away from the garish lights down a dim side street to a decrepit old shop. Through the shop to a room behind - a room that gives the impression of being festooned with cobwebs even if there aren't any actually there. Waiting are another old man and stooped old woman with a face like a bird of prey. Mike looks round the room. A hell of a place for an orgy...

The three old creatures mutter among themselves. Is he dependable? Will he respond? Is he the right material?

"Strong," cackles the old woman appreciatively. "So
strong. The sensation should be wonderful."

Mike is impatient. Where's the action?

The man who brought him here now introduces himself
as Marcus Mesmer. The name means nothing? Ah, how
soon fame dies! Marcus Mesmer and his beautiful
assistant Estelle formed one of the world's greatest
mind-reading teams at the beginning of the century.
Mesmer half bows to his beautiful assistant - the
weird old crone.

Mike is ready to get mad. He didn't come here to
watch some old music-hall illusionist act. And where
does the third character come in: "Is he the one you
send round with the hat?"

There is a threatening silence in the room. All three
of them are sternly concentrating on him. Mike
blinks. He feels dizzy.

Mesmer then solemnly assures him that there were no
illusions in the act. Mesmer and Estelle were - and
are - genuine telepaths, capable of reading other
people's minds. All they lacked in their great days
was the ability to talk back to the minds which they
read - to share sensations to their fullest depth.
But recently they have met Dr. Pokorny here, and when
the three of them bring their united concentration to
bear they can create a whole new fascinating world in
the minds of others.

Create a world...?

Experiences which are dazzling, Mesmer promises.
Ecstasy which is real, yet without dangerous
consequences. Intoxication with no hangover.

Abandonment without any need for remorse.

Kinky dreams? Mike is sceptical.

Mesmer produces a bottle of a dark fluid. It has the property of relaxing the subconscious mind, making it pliable, so that creative influences can work on it, can play on it as on a musical instrument. Before Mike can say scornfully that he has tried, Mesmer goes on to promise that he and his two colleagues will stimulate a range of enthralling sensations in the mind - not the usual dreamy confusion of the drugged imagination, but clearcut, exciting sensations. The subject will see the world in new colours with a new intensity.

Mike decides he's got nothing to lose. He takes a draught of the liquid. It seems to have no effect.

"You may go now," says Mesmer.

"Go? Now, wait a minute. What's the gimmick? Nothing's happening."

"It will. Soon it will begin to work. Go now - and come back here at eight o'clock tomorrow evening."

"The hell with that."

"You will come back here at eight o'clock tomorrow evening." Mesmer commands him.

Mike shrugs and goes out.

The three settle down in their sinister little room, preparing to concentrate. Then decide there must be just a little run-in this evening. They don't want to take risks until they are sure he is susceptible to their control. He mustn't be jarred into consciousness in the middle of some incident. So for this evening they will concentrate on planting enjoyable fantasies in Mike's mind.

Oh, to be as young as he is! The three of them can now live only through the sensations of younger, more vigorous people. All their ecstasies are secondhand. But that's better than experiencing no ecstasy at all.

Outside in the shadowy street, Mike strolls away. His scornful expression begins to relax. He walks past an open doorway and a girl accosts him. Harsh canned music blares out from inside. Mike brushes her off...then looks again.

Suddenly through his eyes we see that she has changed. She has become beautiful, sensuous, enticing. The music is no longer harsh: it has changed to a rhythmic, sensual folk song, a pounding invitation to wild abandonment. Mike follows her in. The rooms inside are lavishly decorated and the music is really good, shading from raucousness into languor. Mike is led through a dream world into a room where he and the girl make love skilfully and magnificently.

And the three old people sit in their cobwebby room in subdued light, smiling in a shared rapture.

The next day Alan asks Mike where he got to last night. Mike can't remember a thing. He has been trying all morning, but it has all faded. All that's left is a feeling that he had a pretty fab time - or a pretty fab dream, maybe.

That evening they meet Penny and go out as usual.
Alan and Penny pull Mike's leg about his loss of
memory. But they don't find it so funny when a drab
girl in a doorway accosts Mike. "Hey - remember me?"
No, he doesn't remember her. She is indignant. "You
had some pretty terrific things to say to me last
night." Penny looks at Mike in disgust.

They are in a club when eight o'clock comes. Mike, a
glazed look in his eye, abruptly says he must leave.
He is gone before they can ask what is wrong. He goes
back to the room where the three are waiting for him.
They give him more of the drug, which he accepts
without hesitation. Then he sets out again into the
streets.

"This time?" says the old crone eagerly.

Mesmer nods. "Yes. This time..."

"I've dreamed about this. So often."

"Now it will be real. Real for us, not for him. He
wouldn't appreciate it."

They laugh savagely. Then they argue as to who is to
be the first to control Mike - the first to make the
choice. Mesmer insists that he brought them together
and planned the whole thing, and that he must have
the first go.

Mike, in his trance, wanders down some back streets.
On a corner a couple of pretty girls are talking -
saying, "Right, well, see you tomorrow" and "Don't
forget" and "All right...goodnight." One girl goes
into a delicatessen while Mike watches her placidly

as though he has all the time in the world. Then she comes out and goes into a house split up into bedsitting-rooms. Mike follows her quietly up the stairs.

As soon as she has gone into one of the rooms, Mike knocks. The girl opens the door. "What is it?" Mike says that he has just moved into one of the rooms upstairs and is out of shillings for the electricity meter. Can she help? He chats her up, and edges his way into her room. As she digs a couple of shillings out of an old coffee tin in the cupboard, Mike watches her... and his face gradually begins to change. We see it becoming the face of Mesmer on Mike's shoulders - but more evil than Mesmer... the basic Mesmer, a face of lust and horror.

The girl turns and sees him. Her smile fades. Before she can scream, Mike puts his hand over her mouth and throws her towards the bed. He begins to strangle her.

The three old ones are enjoying every moment of it. Mesmer's hands clench and unclench as though he were doing the strangling. Certainly he feels every tremor, every thrill through all the nerves of his being. At last he raises one hand in a commanding gesture.

We see Mike making exactly the same gesture as though he were a puppet on a string. He carries the gesture through, reaching up for a knife from the narrow shelf where the girl keeps her few cooking utensils. He brings the knife down, poises it above his head for a moment, and then drives down, stabbing, slashing, hacking.

The face of Mesmer is hideously enraptured. Hammering

guitar chords beat out the rhythm of the attack. And in a swimming, swirling cloud behind Mesmer are the ghostly, remote features of Estelle and Pokorny, nodding in vicarious rapture.

When Mike has finished he lets the knife fall, and goes out of the room and out of the house. In the street he walks calmly away and blends into the shadows.

The newspaper headlines scream: GIRL MURDERED IN FLAT. SADISTIC KILLER AT LARGE.

And a couple of days later there is another: FIENDISH KILLER CARVES AGAIN.

We follow Mike through a series of hideous episodes which mount in tension and viciousness. Every evening he is drawn back to the room where the three are waiting for him, and every evening the dose of drugs is renewed. Alan and Penny cannot understand what happens. On one occasion they try to track him down, but lose him in a maze of back streets. He himself has no recollection later of what has happened during his wanderings. The killings and other incidents are so widely scattered over London that the police can find no logical pattern in them, and Mike has no reason to suppose that he is in any way connected with them.

Each time he walks through a rosy dream, in which everything is distorted into enticing shapes. And each time the reality is terrible - but he is unaware of it.

One intended victim escapes, and Mesmer and his

colleagues decide to lie low for a while. But they
still make Mike come each evening for his injection,
then let him go back to his friends. Alan and Penny
find his manner odd on such occasions, but then Mike
has always been a bit odd.

The evening comes when the deadly trio wish to resume
operations. Mike, Penny and Alan are in a club,
talking about the recent murders to a background of
pulsating music. Penny shivers over the gruesome
details.

Then a girl folk singer in the club starts a sad
ballad about a faithless lover pursued by the ghost
of his dead girl.

It is eight o'clock. Mike goes suddenly stiff and
silent and then gets up to leave. He is 'shushed' by
people all round him who are listening to the singer.
Alan and Penny pull him back into his chair. "But
I've got to go," he insists; "I've got a date." Alan
half-jokingly and half-irritably makes him stay where
he is. The girl goes on singing. "Can't stand that
row," growls Mike." "And that girl...God, she's
awful!" He is getting difficult, wants desperately to
get away.

From a distance, Mesmer and his accomplices feel the
strain. They decide to relax the tension - let Mike
stay where he is for a while rather than arouse the
suspicion of his friends.

Then Estelle says greedily that Mike hates the girl
who is singing the song. The hatred has been formed
because of the tussle in his mind, having to stay
and listen to her when every impulse urged him to

get away. It's Estelle's turn to choose - and her choice is that Mike should make the girl singer the victim tonight. Estelle hates her even more than Mike does: the girl is young and attractive, she has a fine voice, she has all the makings of a future star. And Estelle is faded...finished. Let her have the sensation of killing the girl!

The others agree. But if they bring Mike here to give him a further dose of the controlling drug, by the time he gets back the girl may have gone. His nervous hatred of her is so intense at the moment that they are reluctant to let her slip: they will lose a unique sensation if Mike's fury goes off the boil.

They decide to risk letting him go ahead. The effects of yesterday's dose are still strong. The three of them ought to be able to keep him under telepathic control long enough to accomplish the deed. The challenge is one they can't resist.

In the club, the girl stops singing and gives way to a group. People begin to move about. Mark slips away from his friends. Penny is worried about him and urges Alan to go and see what he's up to. Alan does so and finds Mike smoothly chatting up the girl singer. He comes back to Penny and reports.

"But he said he couldn't stand her!"

"Must be one of those love-hate relationships."

Wryly they quit the club, leaving Mike to his own devices. They play out a sweet-sour little love scene - or the beginning of one. Penny feels peeved about Mike, is fed up with being neglected by him, and is ready to be drawn towards Alan. And Alan is ready to do the drawing. They feel half guilty, half defiant about Mike.

Mike and Laura, the girl singer, leave the club together. Mike talks glibly about a terrific little club on the south bank that hardly anyone knows about yet but where the music is way ahead of the stuff you hear in this part of the town. He half flatters, half challenges the girl until she agrees to come with him and show the folks down there what she can do. Mike hustles her into a taxi.

They leave the taxi in a bleak main road near Waterloo and walk down deserted back streets towards the river near Bankside. The girl begins to have doubts and wants to go back. Mike urges her on. We have a brief flash of it all as it appears to Mike - the lights on the north bank of the river scintillating, the girl beautifully dressed, laughing and smiling at him and swaying towards him...he walks through a slowly shifting dream.

And then the reality. The dark waterside, the black hulk of a barge, the grim surroundings, and a junk heap from which Mike picks up a jagged iron bar.

"Go on - sing!"

The girl is paralysed with fear. Mike advances on her, demanding that she shall sing for him. That's what she came here for, wasn't it? She's young, she's got talent - let's hear her! And as he comes closer, his face changes into a grotesque travesty of Estelle's - leering, envious, spiteful.

The iron bar is raised. "Sing!"

Pitifully, Laura tries to sing a wavering folk song.

"Is that the best you can do?"

Mike swings the bar and strikes Laura a glancing blow that hurls her back against the junk heap. "If you can't do any better than that" - his voice now is Estelle's croaky, vindictive voice - "you don't deserve to have a throat. Or a tongue. Let's cut one and have the other out, shall we? You won't be needing them."

Laura tries to run, but he fells her with a terrific blow, snatches up a jagged piece of metal from the junk, and pounces on her. He turns her body over and forces her mouth open. Then, as he begins to rip her tongue out, his movements weaken. He stops. Estelle's face begins to fade. Mike puts a hand dazedly to his forehead.

And Mesmer, in the room, says desperately: "We can't hold him! The drug is weakening."

"We ought not to have risked it."

"Hold on! Hold him!"

They concentrate, their eyes wide and hideous.

But Mike wakes from his trance and stares in horror at the crumpled mess on the ground. He looks at his bloodied hands. Then the full terror of it hits him. He whimpers, turns and runs madly away.

"Lost him!" breathes Estelle in anguish.

"We'll find him again," Mesmer says reassuringly. "He will come back to us. He will come back to us. He will have to come back."

A newspaper headline in the early evening edition the next day: MANGLED CORPSE IDENTIFIED: FOLK SINGER SLAIN.

Alan is waiting for Penny in a crowded snack bar at lunchtime. He sees the heading and a photograph of the girl and is appalled. When Penny comes in and kisses him gaily, she can't understand his lack of response. Then he shows her the newspaper. They can't believe it...refuse to believe it. It's a coincidence. Mike couldn't have...

Alan telephones the garage where Mike works. He has not been in today and the proprietor hasn't heard a word from him. He's pretty mad about it.

Back in the office where she works, Penny gets a phone call from Mike. He's desperate - in real trouble. He can't tell her over the phone; pleads with her to meet him at once. He gives her details of where he is and how to get there. When Mike has rung off, Penny tries to contact Alan, but he is out on a job and won't be back for an hour or more. She decides to go on her own, begs time off from the office, and leaves.

At the same time Mesmer and his accomplices plan to track down Mike. They no longer have sufficient power to make him come to them, so they must go to him. He must be silenced - not by violence unless absolutely necessary. All they want is to take him under their mental control again. There is no real risk of his blabbing and telling what little he remembers of the truth, and in any case no-one would accept his fantastic story. But it would be embarrassing, might make future operations difficult...and anyway they

don't want to be deprived of their sensual pleasures
for too long.

All three of them concentrate, reaching out mentally
to make what flickering contact is possible with
Mike's mind. They cannot take him over; but they
think they can work out where he is. They set out in
search of him - three grim, shuffling figures
cowering through the streets.

Mike and Penny are in a bare room in a derelict
building - one of the deserted terraces waiting to be
pulled down. Mike is just concluding his explanations
of what has happened. Penny doesn't know whether to
believe him or not. Has he gone insane? But she tries
to calm him and to sympathise with him. He needs help,
and she assures him that she and Alan will give it.

But what can they do? He is a murderer. He sobs that
he can't go on living with the knowledge of what he
has done. Somehow he must destroy the three men who
have led him into this nightmare so that they can
never again lure anyone into their clutches. But
whatever crimes he may have committed under their
spell, he can't kill them in cold blood...and they're
not likely to let him turn on them when he is in one
of his trances! If only there were some way of
striking back at them mentally while under their
control - somehow shattering their minds
telepathically while under their control, while they
are completely engulfed in his own sensations...But
they would surely read his mind and stop him doing
anything?

Penny suggests that he come to her flat that evening,
as the girl who shares it with her is away on
holiday. She will ask Alan to come as well. Then they
can try to work out what to do. Say eight o'clock?

She leaves.

And Mesmer, Estelle and Pokorny, from the shelter of an adjacent derelict building, watch her go.

"If he's talked to her, we'll have to settle her," says Estelle.

Pokorny chuckles. "It is my turn to decide. I choose her as tonight's victim. That would be a pleasant irony, don't you think? If that is his girl friend, it will all have an extra savour to it."

They are delighted by this idea. They close in on the house where the wretched Mike is sheltering. Mesmer and Estelle go warily in. Mike hears them coming and tries to escape but they pen him against one wall of the decrepit landing. As they advance like two vicious animals, Mike warns them that he'll beat them up if they come any closer. Cornered, some of his old bravado comes back.

"Come on! You like pain well enough when it's inflicted on someone else. Do you think you'll enjoy suffering yourself?"

The two stop. Mesmer says that Mike may as well give in. They will claim him in their own good time. He can't escape them now. And why should he want to? Soon perhaps he can pull off a daring robbery under their control...they can all live richly...live for kicks, without danger.

"Without danger to you!" cries Mike. "But what about me?" Half coaxing, half mocking, Mesmer creeps cautiously forward. Just as Mike is about to launch himself at his tormentors, the door immediately beside him is flung open and Pokorny jumps out, pressing a pad over

Mike's mouth. Mike struggles, flounders...sags. And while he is still dazed and half-conscious, Mesmer takes a bottle of the drug from his pocket and administers another dose.

Before Mike can recover and fight back, the three of them scuttle like evil spiders out of the house and over the rubble. Mike takes a few tottering steps down the stairs, trying to shake himself awake.

As they disappear through a gap in a collapsing wall, Mesmer says smugly! "We can claim him when we need him this evening. He's ours again."

Penny phones Alan, only to find that he can't get away early. There is an urgent job which will keep him busy for some hours. But he will be along as soon as possible after eight.

Mike arrives at the flat and Penny lets him in. It is five to eight. They discuss the murdered girls and other recent crimes of terror in which Mike may or may not have been involved. How can he be sure? No finger of suspicion has yet been pointed at him but it soon may be: last night, for instance, there must have been other people at the club who will remember him and may even now be reporting to the police. And the taxi driver may be able to give a description of him. Mike just remembers vaguely that he was taken to the south bank by taxi.

Even if he is not accused, he cannot go on living with such a weight on his conscience.

Penny is still not sure how much of this is the rambling of a pathological killer and how much some

terrible fantasy Mike has built up in his mind. She
tries to persuade him that he must see a doctor. He
won't be brutally treated: a doctor will help to make
him well and will arrange for him to be looked after.
Mike realises that she thinks he is insane and that
he is making up the story of Mesmer and the others.
He rages helplessly at her, and to soothe him she
pretends to believe the story and argues with him on
his own terms. If the drug has worn off, he has
nothing further to fear, has he? If he hasn't seen
Mesmer and has been given no further drug after his
terrible awakening last night...

But he has seen Mesmer, Mike admits. And he has been
given more of the drug. Penny is startled but tries
to remain logical. He has really seen them; yet they
have allowed him to come here and they aren't
stopping him from telling her all these details? Mike
tries to explain the Mesmer is not yet in control of
him: the drug has to take effect. When it does, they
will move into his mind and take over when they have
plans for him. He doesn't know when.

Penny recalls the previous 'possession' fits. They
all started at eight o'clock. And it's almost that
now - only a minute to go.

Alan, on his way to the flat in his rattletrap car,
finds the usual route blocked. A fire is raging
from a building in one of the streets, and it is
necessary to make a detour. He finds himself snarled
up in traffic, and is almost driven on to a pavement
by an approaching fire engine. Glancing impatiently
at his watch he realises that it is just eight
o'clock... and suddenly he feels frightened, stricken
by an unease which he cannot explain. He twists the

car round and desperately seeks the quickest way to
Penny's flat.

Penny is suddenly aware that Mike's tone of voice
is changing. His whole expression chills. She tries
to go on talking reasonable to him - but then she
sees what is happening to his face. Gradually it is
wrinkling and sagging into the features of Pokorny.
Penny tries to scream, but Mike hurls her on the bed
and thrusts a pillow down on her face.

The struggle mounts to a frenzy. Mesmer, Estelle and
Pokorny are utterly absorbed in it. We see Pokorny at
last raise his hand as though seeing something far
away...groping for something out of his reach yet
almost accessible.

Mike reaches for a pair of scissors on the table near
the bed...

As he raises them about the weakening Penny, the door
opens and Alan comes in. He stares, incredulously
then throws himself at Mike. Again the scissors
flash.

"Yes!" breathes Estelle. "We can do it. Both of them
- both! - we can do it."

They concentrate, willing Mike to put up a superhuman
struggle. Alan holds his arm, but Mike fights free
and again lunges with the scissors.

Alan suddenly dodges, allows himself to fall back a
pace, and smashes his right fist straight into Mike's
face. There is a strange, triple moan - anguish
forces from the three old people so sunk in Mike's

sensations that the blow hurts them as much as it hurts Mike.

Pokorny's face blurs, as though trying to escape.

Alan lashes out again.

"Get him out!" orders Mesmer. "There's too much noise - get him away. Make him move!"

They concentrate on forcing Mike out of the room, out of the house at full speed. Alan and Penny dash after him, Alan well in the lead. Mike turns and dashes down a side street, across a road at the end, and down an alley. He is halfway down when he sees a policeman blocking the other end, silhouetted against a weirdly leaping brilliance.

Mike looks back. Alan is hard on his heels, already in the alley.

A policeman has his back to him. Mike goes at him full tilt, knocks him to one side, and stumbles out into a road which is an inferno of brightness and heat. There are shouts all round him.

"Get back...stop that man!"

But the voices are swallowed up in a terrific roar as a wall crumbles and flames come blazing out into the road. Mike throws up his arms and then is engulfed by this sudden rush of fire. He screams - and it is as though three or four people were all screaming at once. He is for a moment a black shape in the flames...then a living torch...then there is nothing but flames across the road.

Alan stops and backs away into the alley. Penny

stumbles up behind him and clings to him, sobbing and
gasping.

"Do you thing it was true? Do you think there really
were those people? And if they were really in control
of him when...when that happened..."

The roaring of the flames dies. The voice of the girl
folk singer, sad and hauntingly far away, takes over.
She is singing the bitter lament we have heard
before. And as it throbs in from the distance, we see
three twisted figures on the floor of that shabby
room - the contorted figures of Mesmer, Estelle and
Pokorny. Their faces are charred into dreadful masks
of black ash...charred into their last hideous
grimaces as they, too, savoured the full sensation of
being burnt to death.

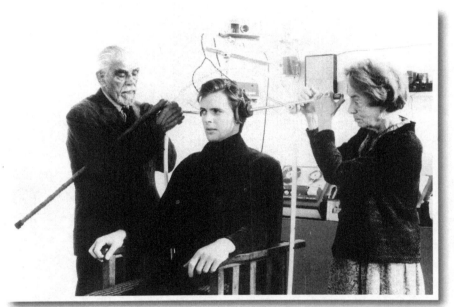

Boris Karloff Ian Ogilvy Catherine Lacey

Catherine Lacey as Estelle Monserrat

Ian Ogilvy and Sally Sheridan

TERROR FOR KICKS

Original story and screenplay

by

John Burke

TERROR FOR KICKS

Original story and screenplay

by

John Burke

David Higham Associates
76 Dean Street
London W1V 6AH

- GENERAL VIEW   EARLY EVENING

ost empty.   SINGER or BAND on
bit hollow.   When title fades
h following interposed scenes:

RLY EVENING

re at the far end of the
fashionable and the sleazy
iana, pseudo Toulouse-Lautrec
gs, kettledrums turned into
e junk of every kind.

of the door with a large
per.   MIKE watches him
never turns too blatantly
t watch and starts to

UMS BASEMENT CLUB. It
ue music.

VENING

with-it dress shop -
e picture is made.
in clothes a couple
ring orders and
ough the window.
kookie but not affectedly
saves, etc. at the window and plucks at
to hemline of a way-out skirt on a dummy
m a steel tape-measure - she measures the distance
a spool and can be snapped back by pressing a
button in the middle of the spool.   She looks up at
BILL for approval: he appraises the result earnestly.

PENNY looks pointedly at her watch.   BILL spreads
his arms in despair and shrugs to say All right, all
right - if you want to go, go.   PENNY drops the tape
spool in her handbag.

5   CREDITS

Behind this batch REGIMS BASEMENT CLUB.   More people
in.   It's beginning slowly to swing.

1   BEHIND MAIN TITLE: INT. BASEMENT CLUB - GENERAL
    VIEW - EARLY EVENING

    At this stage it is almost empty. SINGER or BAND
    on small stage. SOUND a bit hollow. When title
    fades we continue music through following
    interposed scenes:

2   INT. MIKE'S SHOP - EARLY EVENING

    A gimmick gear shop somewhere at the far end of
    the New King's Road, where the fashionable and
    the sleazy mingle. Tarted-up Victoriana, pseudo
    Toulouse-Lautrec posters, birdcages, fire-dogs,
    kettledrums turned into wastepaper baskets,
    expensive junk of every kind.

3   CREDITS

    Behind first batch of credits RESUME BASEMENT
    CLUB. It is beginning to fill up. Continue music.

4   EXT. BILL'S BOUTIQUE - EARLY EVENING
    We see in through the window of a with-it dress
    shop - whatever is the rave at the time the
    picture is made. BILL, a dewy middle-aged
    character in clothes a couple of decades too
    young for him, is waving orders and mouthing
    things we don't hear through the window. PENNY -
    young, smart, a bit kookie but not affectedly so
    - shifts dummies in the window and plucks at
    shoulders, sleeves, etc. She measures the
    distance from floor to hemline of a way-out skirt
    on a dummy with a steel tape-measure - the kind
    that pulls out from a spool and can be snapped
    back by pressing a button in the middle of the
    spool. She looks up at BILL for approval: he
    appraises the result earnestly.

PENNY looks pointedly at her watch. BILL spreads
his arms in despair and shrugs to say ALL right,
all right - if you want to go, go. PENNY drops
the tape spool in her handbag.

5   CREDITS

Behind this batch RESUME BASEMENT CLUB. More
people in. It's beginning slowly to swing.

6   INT. RECORD SHOP - EARLY EVENING

A record spins on a turntable. In a hooded booth
a YOUNG MAN listens. The music is that of the
club, carried through without a break.

ALAN, rather serious but not dull, listening
analytically to the music himself, glances at his
watch and then with a touch of impatience at his
customer.

7   FINAL CREDITS

Finish credits against BASEMENT CLUB GENERAL
VIEW. Bring general hubbub of the club and the
number up loud and the CUT DEAD IN THE MIDDLE OF
BAR.

                                        CUT TO:

8   INT. MESMER'S ROOM

At this stage we see no details of the room. We
have a shock cut to three faces against a dead
white background: MESMER, ESTELLE AND POKORNY.
They are old and seamed - vicious, repellent
faces. No music, no sound until ESTELLE speaks in
a rasping, evil voice.

                         ESTELLE
          Where can we find the right man?
          Who can we use?
                                              CUT TO:

9   INT. BASEMENT CLUB - NIGHT

     LONG SHOT MIKE AND PENNY across the room at a
     table. People jostle to and fro between them and
     CAM. Music takes up again full blast.
                                              CUT TO:

10   INT. BASEMENT CLUB - TWO SHOT MIKE AND PENNY -
     NIGHT

     MIKE is bored. Not ostentatiously yawning but
     remotely, cosmically bored. We should realise as
     we go on that he has practised a pose of non-
     involvement for so long that he has lost the
     ability to relax. He plays abstractedly with
     Penny's steel tape measure. He draws it out,
     snaps it in a few inches at a time by stabbing a
     button.

     PENNY tries to pay attention. She twitches in
     time to the music. PENNY is a girl of wide
     gestures, always on the go, spreading her arms,
     grimacing, bobbing her head - but she must not be
     just an affected, irritating show-off. Her
     exuberance is infectious, even if Mike doesn't
     find it so.

     SINGER or BAND number finishes O.S. SOUND OF
     APPLAUSE O.S

                          PENNY
          Oh, do stop fiddling and give it back.
                     (holds out hand)

MIKE stares at her and deliberately pulls the
tape CUT TO its full length, holding it across
his throat as though to slit it.

>   MIKE
>   Better to end it all now.

>   PENNY
>   Mike...don't fool around. It's quite
>   sharp.

MIKE makes her wait. Then he holds the tape a
fraction of an inch away from him and lets it
whizz shut. PENNY opens her handbag. MIKE tosses
the spool accurately into the bag.

>   MIKE
>   Didn't you want to see if I have real
>   blood in my veins?

>   PENNY
>   I'll bet it's just acid. And that would
>   corrode my tape measure.

>   MIKE
>   So you'd have no way of measuring how
>   far ahead your nose is in the rat race?

MIKE looks away and focuses without any special
interest on something O.S.

                                        PAN TO:

11   INT. BASEMENT CLUB - ANGLE ACROSS ROOM - NIGHT

We pick up a BLONDE CHICK edging her way across
the room and follow her as she passes MIKE and
PENNY. MIKE looks down without any real interest
at her legs.

12 INT. BASEMENT CLUB - ANGLE ON LEGS - NIGHT

Not a prurient shot - just an impression of
shifting legs in op-art stockings, kinky boots,
and so on.

> MIKES (O.S)
> How long d'you think your precious boss
> can last?

> PENNY
> He's lasted nearly fifty years already.

> MIKE (O.S)
> Flagging. Can't keep up with the trends
> for ever.

CUT TO:

13 INT. BASEMENT CLUB - TWO SHOT MIKE AND PENNY -
NIGHT

> PENNY
> Bill doesn't have to keep up with
> them...(flamboyant, 'allez-oop' gesture)
> ...Bill sets them.

> MIKE
> This year, yes. Next year, maybe.
> And after that...?

> PENNY
> All right, Old Mike Moore. What hideous
> future do you predict?

> MIKE
> Five years from now, Bill will be

drawing a pension from the Design
Centre. And you'll be working in a
chain store selling flannel underwear.

                    PENNY
You work wonders for a girl's ego.

                    MIKE
            (waving round room)
Do you think they'll be faithful?
There'll be a new shop, a new name, a
new generation, even. And this little
lot will probably all be married and
settled down by then.

                    PENNY
That's quite in the fashion, too.

                    MIKE
Hinting?

                    PENNY
            (very sharp, defiant)
No.

SINGER or BAND start up new number O.S. MIKE sits
languidly back and stares into middle distance.

14 INT. BASEMENT CLUB - MS SINGER OR BAND - NIGHT

Play as much of new number as desired. Then...

                                        CUT TO:

15 INT. BASEMENT CLUB - ANGLE ON DOOR - NIGHT

ALAN comes into doorway and looks round for his
friends.

16 INT. BASEMENT CLUB - TWO SHOT MIKE AND PENNY -
    NIGHT

PENNY sees Alan and is surprised.

                    PENNY
        Did you know Alan was coming tonight?

                    MIKE
        As I told him we'd be here, I thought
        it was by no means impossibility.
        Why...would you have preferred us to be
        alone together?

                    PENNY
        It would have been an interesting
        experience. Or would it?

                    MIKE
        I get an added frisson from the
        presence of your jealous admirer.

                    PENNY
        For all the frissons I've ever seen you
        get, you might as well be a...a...well,
        a Martian.

                    MIKE
        A Martian...You know, that would
        explain a lot.

PENNY stands up and waves to Alan O.S. Mike sits
back musing.

                    MIKE
        I've always felt I was an alien in this
        odd world. I wonder...

ALAN COMES INTO SHOT.

                    ALAN
          Hello, Mike, Penny. Sorry I'm late.

                    MIKE
          The terrestrial time scale means nothing
          to us Martians.

ALAN is clearly used to this kind of thing. He
grins amiably at Penny and looks round for a
spare chair.

                    PENNY
          I suppose no-one's going to be formal
          enough to ask me to dance?

                    ALAN
          I'm good at the gavotte, and better at
          the bourrée.
                    (puts out his hand to her)
          Shall we-

                    MIKE
                    (getting up)
          Let's move on.

                    ALAN
          But I've only just got here.

                    MIKE
          And if we leave now, you'll be spared
          the disillusion of knowing just how
          awful it is here tonight.

                    PENNY
          But where are we going?

MIKE

Anywhere. Perhaps in the next place
we'll find joy... and beauty... and
liberation.

ALAN

Oh. It's going to be one of those
evenings, is it?

MIX TO:

17 EXT. PUB DOORWAY - NIGHT

MIKE is holding the door open. He bows solemnly
as PENNY and ALAN come out on to the pavement.

MIKE

That elderly female who said (Mimics
voice:) "I've had this stomach since the
day I was born"...do you suppose there's
a seven-year replacement for most people
on the National Health nowadays?

ALAN

The beer in there was pretty awful,
wasn't it?

PENNY
(grimly)
All right. Where next?
    (she hams up cheerfulness)
They say you can find everything you
want in London. If you know where to
look.

MIKE

At this very moment I have no doubt
some exclusive little group somewhere is
sitting down to a cannibal dinner.

49

Everything you want...
(voice rises mockingly yet with a
genuine plea that is unnerving)
Why do I never find anything I want?

The three of them move off along the pavement.

MIX TO:

18   EXT. CINEMA ENTRANCE - NIGHT

ALAN, MIKE AND PENNY stroll aimlessly towards us
and draw level with a lurid poster, as bosomy as
possible. Beside it is a GIRL, obviously waiting
for a boy friend. MIKE stops right in front of
her and stares until the GIRL becomes uneasily
aware of him.

                    MIKE
          Sorry to trouble you, but I'm collecting
          statistics for a public opinion poll.
          (glances meaningly at poster)
          Vital statistics.

                    GIRL
     (suspicious but flattered, preens herself)
          Well , I don't know, I'm sure...what
          sort of thing do you want to know?

                    MIKE
          Oh, so many things. Now, as a human
          being? - you are what is known as a
          human being? Yes. Good. Tell me -

                    GIRL
          Where's your notebook?

                    MIKE
          People from my planet have memories like

tape recorders. Does away with pencil
and paper.

ALAN (in b.g)
Mike, do come along...

GIRL
Look here, what poll did you say you
were on?

MIKE
I didn't. But I will tell you in
confidence that I represent a leading
Market Research Body.

GIRL
I don't like talk about bodies. It's
not right. Or all that about vital
statistics. I know what you're after.
I'm no fool.
PENNY
Mike...please...

GIRL
(to ALAN)
You want to keep an eye on him. He'll
get a punch in the nose if my boy
friend comes along.

MIKE
The pleasure of experiencing pain! Oh,
the pleasure of experiencing anything!

MIX TO:

19 EXT. COFFEE BAR DOORWAY -NIGHT

TRACK with ALAN, MIKE and PENNY as they walk
away along pavement.

                    ALAN
                 (exasperated)
          All right - the Eight Beat Club, then?

MIKE grimaces - bored and dispariging.
They approach the corner of the street.
ALAN and PENNY are getting more and more fed up.

                    ALAN
          We could go and eat at the Unicorn.

                    MIKE
          Beans on toast and Algerian burgundy?

MIKE stops under a lamp at the corner. The side
turning is dark.

                    PENNY
          Mike, can't you ever relax and just let
          things happen? Can't you bear to see
          anyone having any fun?

                    MIKE
          Fun?

                    ALAN
          You're just not with it, are you?

                    MIKE
                 (solemnly)
          I am the 'it' that everyone wants to be
          with.

                    PENNY
          Not me.

                 (to Alan)
          I'm hungry. Shall we go and eat?

                    ALAN
        (glances at MIKE, hesitates, then:)
        Yes. Fine.

                    MIKE
        At last - a new sensation - deserted by
        my friends! I must get the full bitter
        savour of it.

20 EXT. STREET OF CLUBS AND CAFES - ANGLE ALONG
    PAVEMENT - NIGHT

    ALAN and PENNY walk away, glancing back in the
    hope that MIKE will change his mind. MIKE stays
    under the lamp.

                    MIKE
            (calling after them)
        If you find anything really out of the
        ordinary, do let me know. Poste Restante
        St. Jude will find me.

21 EXT. STREET - TWO SHOT ALAN AND PENNY - NIGHT

                    PENNY
        St Jude?

                    ALAN
        The patron saint of lost causes.
                                        CUT TO:

22 EXT. CLOSE SHOT OF WHEELCHAIR - NIGHT

    The WHEEL rolls along the pavement, gleaming in
    the uncertain light. TRACK with it to the corner
    of the street and stop with it as it stops by
    Mike's leg.
                                    CAM FAST UP TO:

                        53

23   CU MESMER

Predatory face, gloating, turned upwards to look
at Mike O.S. Very still, calculating, menacing.

                              CAM PULL BACK TO:

24   EXT. STREET - TWO SHOT MIKE AND MESMER - NIGHT
     MIKE becomes aware of the still, brooding
     presence. He looks down.

                    MESMER
          You're bored, young man.

MIKE raises a supercilious eyebrow does not speak.

                    MESMER
          I could offer you an unusual evening.

                    MIKE
          I doubt it. Some extraordinary
          experiences. Blackcurrant juice and a
          couple of faded blondes?

                    MESMER
          Nothing as dull as that.

                    MIKE
          Blue films? Not for me. I find telly
          commercials much more suggestive.

                    MESMER
          Better that that, I promise you.
                    MIKE
          Drugs? They're not worth the trouble.

                    MESMER
          This will be worth the trouble.

                         54

MIKE looks along the street.

25 EXT. STREET OF CLUBS AND CAFES - MIKE'S P.O.V - NIGHT

A few dismal lights. Glare from the cinema. Not many people about.

>   MESMER (O.S.)
>   There isn't anything else you really
>   want to do then?

26 CU MIKE

MIKE slowly shakes his head, more to himself than to Mesmer. He looks down at Mesmer O.S.

>   MIKE
>   All right. Lead me to it.

27 EXT. DARK SIDE TURNING - LONG SHOT DOWN STREET - NIGHT

MIKE walks slowly beside MESMER in the wheelchair and they blur into the shadows.

FADE TO BLACKNESS

28 INT. DOOR INTO MESMER'S ROOM - NIGHT

This door opens suddenly as a rectangle of light in the blackness. Silhouettes of MIKE and MESMER move through it into the room beyond.

29 INT. MESMER'S ROOM - MESMER'S P.O.V. - NIGHT

Very plain , very scruffy. A dismal little dump. A few chairs. A battered table. ESTELLE and

POKORNY are seated behind the table, waiting for
us. They are both ancient grotesques - sinister
grotesques. We approach them as though in the
wheelchair ourselves, and stop on:

30 CU ESTELLE

She is staring at us, her mouth working.

> ESTELLE
> So you found someone...

31 INT. MESMER'S ROOM - GENERAL VIEW - NIGHT

MIKE stands beside MESMER in the wheelchair and
looks sceptically round the room.

> MIKE
> Bring on the dancing girls.

> POKORNY
> Is he dependable?

> MESMER
> We shall have to try him out.

> ESTELLE
> (greedily leaning across table
>   and gloating over MIKE)
> So strong. The sensations should be
> wonderful.

> MIKE
> Quite a place you have here.
> Just the setting for an orgy.

> MESMER
> Let me introduce myself and my colleagues.

MESMER begins to drive his wheelchair round the
room as he speaks, encircling MIKE, ESTELLE and
POKORNY - rather as though he were creating a
magic circle.

                    MESMER
        I am...Marcus Mesmer.

Mike shrugs.

                    MESMER
        The name means nothing to you?

                    MIKE
        Less than that.

                    ESTELLE
        How soon fame dies!

                    MESMER
        The world's greatest mind-reading team
        of the century - or any other
        century...Marcus Mesmer and his
        beautiful ESTELLE.

MESMER half-bows from his wheelchair at the awful
crone, ESTELLE.

                    MIKE
        You mean you've dragged me here just to
        watch some ancient music-hall
        illusionist act?

                    ESTELLE
        There were never any illusions in our
        act. We are genuine telepaths: we can
        read other people's minds.

                    MIKE
          If you know what was in mine right now
          you'd be throwing the furniture at me.
                    (nods at POKORNY)
          And your friend here - he goes round
          with the hat?

The three of them study him grimly. He shifts
uneasily in spite of himself and glances at the
door.

                    MESMER
          All we lacked in our great days was the
          ability to talk back to the minds with
          which we were in contact. We could not
          share our own sensations or offer mental
          guidance to our contacts. But recently
          we had the good fortune to meet kindred
          talent in Dr Pokorny here. When the
          three of us bring our united
          concentration to bear, we can create a
          whole new fascinating world of
          experience.

                    MIKE
          Create a world?

32 CU MESMER

He is staring fanatically into the unknow.
                    MESMER
          Dazzling, indescribable experiences.
          Ecstasty which is real, yet without
          dangerous consequences. Intoxication
          with no hangover. Abandonment with no
          need for remorse.

MESMER looks up now, commandingly, at Mike O.S.

33 TWO SHOT MESMER AND MIKE

MIKE looking down at MESMER in the wheelchair.

                    MIKE
      Kinky dreams?

MESMER looks past him and nods an order to
Pokorny O.S.

34 INT. MESMER'S ROOM - GENERAL VIEW - NIGHT

POKORNY comes round the table with a small
bottle.

                    POKORNY
      This fluid has the property of relaxing
      the conscious mind - making it pliable
      so that creative influences can work on
      it.
                    ESTELLE
      We can play on it as on a musical
      instrument.

                    MIKE
      And you think you're going to use me as
      bagpipes?
                    MESMER
                 (earnestly)
      I promise that my colleagues and I will
      take you out of your normal restricted
      self and stimulate a range of
      enthralling sensations such as you have
      never known before.

Mike doesn't believe a word of it. But he'll

try anything once. He takes the bottle from
POKORNY.

                    MIKE
    No glass? Never mind - from the bottle.

Mike tips back the contents of the bottle. The
three of them watch him, tense. Mike waits for
results.

                    MESMER
    You may go now.

                    MIKE
    Go? But what about the multi-coloured
    miracles you promised? Nothing's
    happening.

                    MESMER
    Soon it will begin to work. Go now -
    and be back here at nine o'clock
    tomorrow evening.

                    MIKE
    Complete change of programme tomorrow?
    There'd need to be before you'd get me-

35 CU MESMER

                    MESMER
                  (viciously)
    You will come back here at nine o'clock
    tomorrow evening.

36 INT. MESMER'S ROOM - ANGLE ON MIKE FROM BEHIND
    TABLE - NIGHT

POKORNY moves round to resume his seat so that

POKORNY and ESTELLE have their backs to us and we
see Mike between their heads. Mike sizes them all
up, then shrugs.

> MIKE
> Thanks for the barley water. It was
> just what I needed.

Mike turn and goes out.

37   EXT. STREET OF CLUBS AND CAFES - NIGHT

Mike stops on corner as before. He looks from
side to side. Nothing has changed. He grimaces
and moves on.

38   INT. MESMER'S ROOM - NIGHT

MESMER runs his wheelchair close up to the other
two.
> MESMER
> This evening we will have only a run-
> in. Not too bold. Not the first time.

> POKORNY
> I agree. We must be sure we can control
> him.

> MESMER
> Shall we concentrate, then?

They move into a little huddle, their heads
coming close together.

> ESTELLE
> Oh, to be as young and **** as he is
> instead of taking our ecstasies at
> second-hand!

MESMER
Better than experiencing no ecstasy at
all. And safer.
(POKORNY AND ESTELLE chuckle and nod)
Much safer...for us.

39   EXT. STREET OF CLUBS AND CAFES - NIGHT

MIKE approaches slowly. He comes level with an
open doorway. A blotchy, heavily made up girl,
RACHEL, leans out.

SOUND O.S. - a gust of canned music from inside.

RACHEL
Hey - want some fun?

Mike stops and leans on wall (or railing), but
only out of boredom. He is ready to move on.

MIKE
I'd love a closely fought game of
chess.

RACHEL
Aw, come on, lover - don't be that way.

MIKE is about To push himself upright and walk
away. Then he blinks and stares at her. He puts
his hand across his eyes.

CUT TO:

40   CU MESMER

Eyes wide, staring, jubilant - urging something.

CUT TO:

41   EXT. STREET OF CLUBS AND CAFES - NIGHT

Open full on doorway, MIKE'S P.O.V. RACHEL is in exactly the same pose as in SC. 39 but is quite changed. She is a beautiful girl, glamorously dressed. Her voice is no longer harsh but mellow and inviting.

> RACHEL
> Coming to dance with me?

42 INT. DRINKING CLUB ROOM - NIGHT

Use one corner of the room only - a table close to the inner door. A sleazy girl sits with her elbow on the table. MUSIC raucous. MIKE and RACHEL (RACHEL ugly as before) come in. MIKE looks round the room.

43 INT. DRINKING CLUB ROOM- MIKE'S P.O.V. - NIGHT

From this p.o.v. the room is bare save for richly coloured hangings. RACHEL (beautiful again) sways into shot, her arms held out invitingly. MUSIC becomes rich and plushy.

44 INT. DRINKING CLUB ROOM - MIKE'S P.O.V. - NIGHT

MIKE and RACHEL dance. The atmosphere should be as hazy and dreamlike as possible. MIKE'S face is, for the first time, relaxed and contented.

(This scene can be played as far as it will go, with all the implications we need to imply. The dancing can become passionate, the movement suggestive - or we can simply let them sway rhythmically together and let the audience add what they choose to the story.)

MIX TO:

45   INT. MESMER'S ROOM- NIGHT

CLOSE on the heads of MESMER, ESTELLE and
POKORNY, swaying to the same rhythm, their eyes
glazed.

                                        SLOW FADE

                                        FADE IN:

46   INT. BILL'S BOUTIQUE - DAY

PENNY has just finished serving a GIRL CUSTOMER
and is handing her change. GIRL CUSTOMER leaves.
ALAN stands at one side waiting to talk to PENNY.
BILL stands by the door, fawning mockingly over
GIRL CUSTOMER and somehow charming her as she
goes out.
PENNY takes a yellow cloak from the counter and
goes to racks to hand it up. Suddenly she veers
and drapes it over ALAN'S shoulders, then skips
back to get a good look, just as BILL turns back
into the shop.

                    PENNY
                  (to Bill)
        Can you tell boys from butter?
BILL winces and pretends not to be involved. ALAN
slips cloak from his shoulders. PENNY hangs it
up.

It may be possible to play this scene in and
around the clothes and window dummies, with BILL
eavesdropping and then looking loftily
indifferent - resenting ALAN'S presence yet
wishing to be terribly, terribly civilised. He
deplores PENNY'S skittishness as she puts various
bits of gear on ALAN'S head: she is always on the
move, not to twee, but light-hearted and

                        64

affectionate towards ALAN and pleasantly mocking towards BILL.

                    ALAN
          Any word from Mike?

                    PENNY
          Not yet.

                    ALAN
          Perhaps he's ashamed of himself.

                    PENNY
          Oh, he's never ashamed. Even when he
          apologises for something you feel it's
          part of the ritual - just put in to
          balance up.

                    ALAN
          A modulation into the relative major?

                    PENNY
          If you say so. Come to think of it, why
          aren't you at the college this morning?
          You ought to be halfway through the
          Moonlight Sonata by now.
                    ALAN
          All the lecture rooms are being used
          for examinations for two days. I can
          practise at home in the evening, when I
          feel like it.

                    PENNY
          When you feel like it...!

BILL tries to indicate that she should give him a
hand with rearranging stock on the racks. She
nods obediently and sets to work mechanically,

continuing to talk to ALAN over her shoulder.
BILL sees no reason why he should not listen to
such a public discussion.

>   PENNY
> And how often do you feel like it in
> the evening, after all those hours in
> that record shops?

>   ALAN
> Don't say 'that record shop' in that
> tone of voice. You spend enough time
> there scrounging a free listen to all
> the latest discs.

BILL nods vigorous agreement. They both ignore
him.

>   PENNY
> It's all right for me. I can waste my
> time any way I want. I'm not a
> potential genius.

>   BILL
> (unable to repress it, nodding at ALAN)
> Is he?
>   PENNY
> I don't know.

>   ALAN
> Nor do I. And Mike...?

>   BILL
> Your friend Mike will never be satisfied
> with being less than a genius. His
> trouble is he doesn't know what to be a
> genius at.

PENNY spins a black and white leather hat on a
stand so that it revolves like a gramophone
record.

MIX TO:

47   EXT. PAVEMENT - DAY

CLOSE SHOT wheel of wheelchair running along
pavement. It swerves on a corner.

48   EXT. GREENGROCER'S SHOP - DAY

A corner shop with a couple of trestles sticking
out across the pavement, packed with boxes of
fruit and vegetables. GREENGROCER is just going
inside, into the shop itself.

MESMER comes round the corner and tries to
swerve away from the protruding trestles. He
jars his shoulders against a box, the wheelchair
bumps away at an angle , and box of tomatoes
tips over. Tomatoes roll across the pavement
into the gutter.

GREENGROCER comes furiously out of the shop.

                    GREENGROCER
What the hell d'you think you're at?

                    MESMER
          (shakily rubbing shoulder)
This is a very dangerous place to -

                    GREENGROCER
Why don't you look where you're ruddy
well going? It should be illegal to
drive one of them things along the
pavement.

                    MESMER
Those boxes of yours are causing an
obstruction.

                  GREENGROCER
Obstruction? I'll flaming well obstruct
you. Why don't you send someone along
in front of you with a red flag?

GREENGROCER angrily kicks some tomatoes into the
gutter and drags the box out of the way. When he
straightens up he is grumbling on and on as a
matter of principle.

                  GREENGROCER
A good fifteen bobs' worth ruined. No -
nearer a quid, I reckon. All because
you go racketing around like a kid with
a new scooter.

                    MESMER
              (becoming menacing)
I'm not used to being spoken to like
that.

                  GREENGROCER
No? Well that's just too bad, isn't it?
(tries to control himself, begins to
feel a bit ashamed, tries to finish the
whole thing)
Look...sorry, grandad. Let's just
square it up right and proper, and
there's no harm done, eh? Call it a
quid.

                    MESMER
If I find your filthy boxes have damaged
my wheelchair...

GREENGROCER
Now look, mate - are you going to pay?

49 CU MESMER

MESMER
(savagely)
No. You're going to pay.

50 EXT. GREENGROCER'S SHOP - DAY

MESMER swings his wheelchair round and bends over
the wheels to start the chair moving.

51 CLOSE SHOT WHEEL OF WHEELCHAIR - DAY

Wheel begins to turn slowly on pavement. It comes
slowly against a large, ripe tomato. As the wheel
moves, the tomato splits and gushes a red mess
over the pavement.

MIX TO:

52 INT. BILL'S BOUTIQUE - DAY

Start close on swirling red dress to match tomato
in SC.51, then PULL BACK to show PENNY hanging
dress up. BILL comes up to speak to her, but ALAN
has nerved himself to say:

ALAN
I was wondering if you'd like to come
out this evening.

PENNY turns doubtfully towards him. BILL wavers,
then shrugs in tolerant despair and turns towards
the back of the shop.

BILL
(at door to back room)

Two's company. Three's a French farce.
                    (exits)

                    ALAN
I'll meet you in the pub across the
road. We can have a drink and then go
to that new French film...
(the echo makes him glance belatedly
after Bill)
...at the Academy. The last full show
is at 7.30. The film itself is at 8.50,
if you'd sooner eat first.

                    PENNY
You seem to have checked up.

                    ALAN
But if you'd sooner eat afterwards, we
could go to the trattoria down the
road.

                    PENNY
You've got it all worked out?
                    ALAN
Better than shambling about the streets
without a clue what to do, isn't it?

                    PENNY
It'd certainly make a change. But...
Bill did ask me to try to sort out some
new orders this evening - and I'm
supposed to balance the books,
and...well...what's this film about?

                    ALAN
It's a psychological study of two
repressed sisters in a provincial town
during the war.

                    PENNY
          Sounds fun.
                  (tentatively)
          You do take things seriously, don't you?

                    ALAN
          There's quite a lot of fun to be had,
          being serious.

                    PENNY
          Yes. Yes, I know. But try telling that to -

TELEPHONE RINGS, cutting her short. ALAN and
PENNY glance at each other, both sensing who it
will be. PENNY lifts the receiver.

                    PENNY
          BILL'S Pop-Line here...Oh. Yes...
          I thought it might be...I wondered...
          (nods confirmation at ALAN as she listens)
          But where did you get to in the end?
                                          CUT TO:
53 CU MIKE AT TELEPHONE - DAY

                    MIKE
          Believe it or not, I don't remember a
          thing. All I'm conscious of is that
          the...hm...the aftertaste of something
          rather splendid. Very hard to describe.

                                          CUT TO:

54 INT. BILL'S BOUTIQUE - DAY

                    PENNY
                  (into phone)
          I've never known you at a loss for
          descriptive words before...I'm?

                      71

PENNY listens for a few seconds while ALAN, slightly despondent, turns away in polite withdrawal from a private conversation.

> PENNY
> Well, I don't know. I...no, you needn't do that. He's here right now.
> (to ALAN)
> Mike wants us to meet him this evening. Usual place. Usual time.

ALAN turns to face her. They both look sheepish.

> ALAN
> No hard work on the order books?

> PENNY
> (covering telephone mouthpiece)
> No piano practice...and no French film?

> ALAN
> Doesn't look like it, does it?
> (pause, both of them undecided
> yet knowing it's inevitable)
> Why do we put up with him? Why do we come running whenever he snaps his fingers?

> PENNY
> Because...well, because he's Mike.
> (into phone)
> All right. We'll see you then.

55 INT. BASEMENT CLUB - NIGHT

LONG SHOT across club to MIKE, PENNY and ALAN at a table. MIKE is talking volubly while the other two look incredulous.

INT. BASEMENT CLUB - GROUP SHOT - NIGHT

Angled on MIKE as he finished what he has been
saying.

                MIKE
...and from the time you left me on
that corner I don't remember a thing.

               PENNY
But it's so spooky. You must have some
idea what you did.

                MIKE
Not a flicker.

               PENNY
But you could have done something
terrible.
                MIKE
Not yet.
(his own words surprised him. An awkward pause)
I have an odd feeling it isn't ended.
I'm...waiting...for something to
happen.
      (tries to laugh it off in his
      old manner but doesn't succeed)
But I've been waiting all my life. No
reason why it should begin to happen
now.

               ALAN
You certainly found some stronger booze
than the stuff we started on last
night.

MIKE'S head clicks down almost mechanically as he
looks at his watch. He begins to get up.

                        PENNY
            Wanderlust again?

                        MIKE
            See you.
                        ALAN
            In view of your pressing invitation to
            us to tag along...

                        MIKE
            Stay where you are. I...don't think
            I'll be long.

MIKE makes a path through the dancers.

                        ALAN
            I don't like it. It's somehow...
            sinister.
                        PENNY
            Anyone for menace?
                                            CUT TO:

57 CU TABLE IN MESMER'S ROOM - NIGHT

POKORNY's hand comes into shot and places bottle
on table. Hand is withdrawn. MIKE's hand comes
into shot and picks up the bottle.
                                            CUT TO:

58 CU MIKE

MIKE tips the bottle back and drains it.
                                            CUT TO:
59 INT. BASEMENT CLUB - NIGHT

ALAN and PENNY dancing. They enjoy it without
making too violent an exhibition. As they come
together and separate, in whatever the up-to-the-

                        74

minute steps are, they fling remarks at each
other.

> PENNY
> Better than playing scales?

> ALAN
> I'm on to chords now - ten fingers at a
> time.

> PENNY
> Making with the Beethoven, huh?

> ALAN
> Never cared for the man. Now <u>Bach</u>...

> PENNY
> What's so special about Bach?

> ALAN
> If you got to be told, you ain't got it.

> PENNY
> Tell me all the same.

They dance towards the door. As they approach it,
MIKE appears in the doorway. He looks thoughtful,
remote. PENNY sees him and draws ALAN's attention
to him. MIKE's presence is a magnet. They are
drawn towards him.

60 INT. BASEMENT CLUB - ANGLE ON DOORWAY - NIGHT

> PENNY
> Had a nice think?

> MIKE
> I don't know.

                    ALAN
Where've you been this time?

                    MIKE
I don't know.

                    PENNY
Perhaps the most brilliant
conversationalist of our time.

                    MIKE
It's just like last night. And I still
have this feeling that I have only to
wait a little while and something will
happen.

              PENNY and ALAN
              (in mocking chorus)
But I've been waiting all my life.
No reason why it should begin to happen
now.

MIKE looks into the room and then turns away -
not with distance but with complete indifference,
as though he doesn't belong here and can't be
bothered to make conventional noises. He leaves.
ALAN and PENNY exchange glances of concern and
follow him. MIKE stops, puzzled by something
that's going on inside.

              MESMER'S VOICE
                    (O.S)
              (very croaky and resonant)
The night is young.

                    ALAN
What did you say?

                    MIKE
        Was that me? It sounded like 'the night
        is young'.

                    PENNY
        Very original.

                    ALAN
                (to PENNY)
        I'll see you home.

                    MIKE
        Getting to be a habit, isn't it?

                    PENNY
        Well, since you don't...

MIKE cuts her off in mid-sentence by turning and
walking off. He raises his hand in an airy
gesture of dismissal.
                                        CUT TO:

60A CU MIKE'S HAND - EXT

It waves slowly, derisively, stroking the air.
                                        CUT TO:
60B CU MIKE'S HAND - INT.

The hand is now on girl's back, making the same
stroking motion.

MUSIC IN SLOW AND SMOOCHY

CAM PULLS BACK to show MIKE and LANGUID GIRL
dancing in a discotheque. MIKE's head droops on
to her bare shoulder.
                                        CUT TO:
60C CU MESMER

MESMER's head droops in echo of MIKE's. He sighs.

CUT TO:

60D INT. DISCOTHEQUE (OR CLUB) - NIGHT

MIKE is dancing fiercely but gracefully with
ANOTHER GIRL.

MUSIC IN LOUD AND FAST - complete change of
tempo.

CUT TO:

60E CU ESTELLE

ESTELLE's head jerks to and fro in a grotesque
ragtime parody of SC. 60D. She gets more and more
tired and erratic but cannot stop. We fade very
slowly on her.

SLOW FADE
FADE IN:

60F EXT. ALL-NIGHT COFFEE STALL - NIGHT

This could be on Embankment or Convent Garden.
MIKE is leaning alone against one end of the
stall, sipping hot coffee. Well-dressed DRIP and
DEB come to counter. DRIP is paralytic, can
hardly speak. DEB glances at MIKE. MIKE lifts cup
in salute and gives almost imperceptible jerk of
his head. DEB sees that her boy friend the DRIP
is nearly asleep as he tries to give his order,
and she edges along towards MIKE. MIKE takes a
brandy flask from his pocket, puts his cup down
on the counter. He pours brandy into his cup and
into a presumably empty cup near it. They both
raise their cups and look blearily into each
other's eyes.

60G INT. MESMER'S ROOM - NIGHT

MESMER, ESTELLE AND POKORNY dead beat. POKORNY
winces at the impact of the brandy, and puts his
hand to his throat. Gradually he forces himself
out of his trance of concentration and looks
wearily at the other two.

> POKORNY
> I'm tired. I can't keep this up.

> ESTELLE
> (jolted from her trance, yawning)
> I'm not so much tired as bored.

> MESMER
> (offended)
> Bored?

> ESTELLE
> It's the same thing over and over
> again. I want more than that. A lot
> more. Use him!

> POKORNY
> Let's call it a day.

> ESTELLE
> (laughing harshly at this
> memory of an earlier remark)
> The day is young.

> MESMER
> Exactly. This is no time for sleep. If
> you want more...you shall have more. I
> know just the thing.

61 EXT. STREET OF CLUBS AND CAFES - NIGHT

ALAN, MIKE and PENNY strolling aimlessly, not at
ease with one another.

                    PENNY
          Of course you could be the eccentric
          son of a duke. Bouts of amnesia.
          Occasional fits of lucidity -

                    ALAN
          Not that I've noticed.

They draw level with door of club in which RACHEL
stands, hopefully looking out for custom. She
stares at MIKE and recognises him. As he walks
slowly past she grows peeved.

                    RACHEL
          Hey, lover - remember me?

They all look back. MIKE stares at her with
insulting lack of recognition.

                    RACHEL
          Honest...nothing to say to me?

                    MIKE
          Nothing you'd care to hear, my pet.

                    RACHEL
          Gawd, I ask you! You had some pretty
          terrific things to say last night. And
          more besides. Talk about actions
          speaking louder than words...!

MIKE looks at her with disbelief and contempt,
and moves on. CAM TRACKS with the three. PENNY

looks at MIKE in disgust.

>   ALAN
>   No wonder you prefer to forget.
>   (To MIKE)
>   Let's call it a day, shall we?

>   PENNY
>   Is that what you'd call it?

                                    FADE IN:

62 EXT. GREENGROCER'S SHOP - DAY

It is early morning and there's nobody about. The
pavement is deserted and all the trestles and
boxes are inside the shop. CAM PULLS BACK to take
in deserted length of street. A truck approaches
and stops at the kerb. The GREENGROCER gets out
and begins to unload boxes from back of truck.
(Perhaps insert:
62A.   CU of box with part of a name and the
        words 'COVENT GARDEN' on it)

GREENGROCER carries two or three piled boxes to
door of shop.

63 EXT. GREENGROCER'S SHOP - ANGLE ON DOOR - DAY

GREENGROCER takes out key and opens door. He
picks up boxes and shuffles into interior.

MIKE comes into shot - back view only - with a
heavy spanner in his right hand. He goes quickly
into shop.

64 INT. GREENGROCER'S SHOP - DAY

Space is congested with trestles and boxes

waiting to be put out on pavement. Shelves and
tilted boxes fruit and vegetables round walls.

GREENGROCER wriggles a path between obstructions
and lowers boxes he is carrying to the floor, or
on to the counter. As he straightens up, SOUND OF
DOOR SLAMMING behind him. He turns.

65 INT. GREENGROCER'S SHOP - ANGLE ON MIKE - DAY

Mike is standing with his back to the closed
door. Light through window falls on his head and
face. He wears a stocking mask to distort his
features. He move forward slowly with the spanner
in his hand. Both he and GREENGROCER behave for a
few moments as though hypnotised - as though
moving through treacle. There is a slow night-
marish quality about this before violence breaks
loose.

> GREENGROCER
> What the hell are you doing here?

MIKE comes plodding on. GREENGROCER edges along
with back to the counter, squeezing between
boxes. MIKE tracks him dispassionately between
the boxes.

> GREENGROCER
> If you don't get out of here...
> Look, I'm warning you...

> MIKE
> (brief puzzlement uncertainty)
> I don't want...I don't know what I...

CUT TO:

66 CU MESMER

MESMER is staring fixedly ahead. He licks his
lips.

                    MESMER
        Hold him! Hold him! Concentrate!
        (A BEAT MESMER slowly raises his right
            arm as though clutching something)
        Now...!

                                        CUT TO:

67 CU GREENGROCER

He is staring upwards at an angle, not believing
what he sees.

                                        CUT TO:

68 CU MIKE'S GLOVED RIGHT HAND

MIKE is holding the spanner aloft. It is poised
for a second and then it comes down. GREENGROCER
SCREAMS O.S

                                        CUT TO:

69 INT. GREENGROCCER'S SHOP - GENERAL VIEW - DAY

There is a flight round the shop, in and out of
the boxes. Maybe handheld camera - dodging,
reeling, all over the place. GREENGROCER sobs,
trying to crawl away. MIKE stumbles against
boxes, jars his elbow, misses some of his blows.
The two of them stagger in and out of the light
from the window.

70 INT. GREENGROCER'S SHOP - ANGLE DOWN THROUGH
    CHAOS ON GREENGROCER - DAY

GREENGROCER is on his knees, pinned against a box
with no escape. He stares up imploringly.

GREENGROCER
Why pick on me? What've I ever done to
you...?

The box is suddenly kicked away so that he falls,
rolling over. MIKE's left hand comes into frame
and grabs his shoulder, turning him to face
upwards.

CUT TO:

71 CU MESMER

MESMER looks from side to side. CAM PULLS BACK to
take in ESTELLE and POKORNY. They also look from
side to side as though sizing up a room and
making a choice.

ESTELLE lifts one hand and points.

CUT TO:

72 INT. GREENGROCER'S SHOP - MS MIKE - DAY

MIKE reaches out as though his arm were jerked by
a puppet string. He grabs the corner of tilted
box of oranges and drags them from the shelf.
CRASH O.S as box falls and shatters.

CUT TO:

73 CU POKORNY

POKORNY points in opposite direction.

CUT TO:

74 INT. GREENGROCER'S SHOP - MS MIKE - DAY

MIKE wrenches shelving away so that boxes
collapse all round him.

75　INT. GREENGROCER'S SHOP - GENERAL VIEW - DAY

GREENGROCER struggles up to his knees. MIKE
flails out and knocks him into the middle of the
debris.

76　EXT. GREENGROCERS SHOP AND PAVEMENT - DAY

Truck is in shot at kerb. POLICEMAN comes up and
stops truck. Hears NOISE OF SPLINTERING WOOD O.S.
Turns towards shop door. NOISE comes and door
opens. MIKE, still wearing stockings, framed in
doorway. POLICEMAN hurries towards him. Mike
turns and slams door, going back in.

77　INT. GREENGROCER'S SHOP - GENERAL VIEW - DAY

GREENGROCER huddled in wreckage, sobbing. MIKE
stumbles past him and wrenches inner door open.
He goes through.

78　INT - MESMER'S ROOM - DAY

MESMER, ESTELLE and POKORNY sit back and sigh
with satisfaction.

> POKORNY
> Exhausting.

> ESTELLE
> But delightful.

> MESMER
> A most rewarding experience. The feel of
> things coming apart under one's
> fingers...
> 　　　　(flexes his fingers)

                              POKORNY
Perhaps one of us ought to have been in
the greengrocer's mind - just to
experience his reaction.

                              MESMER
Too complicated. And very dangerous. My
heart isn't what it was.

                              ESTELLE
And the next step - ultimate experience?
You think this evening...?

                              MESMER
Patience...patience! We musn't use our
young friend up too quickly. Perhaps at
the weekend, as a special treat, do you
think?

They sigh, a long sigh of satisfaction that
hisses over through.
                                        MIX TO:

79   EXT. AN ALLEYWAY - DAY

Mike walks briskly but in no panic down alleyway.
His stocking mask and gloves have gone. He looks
quite carefree.
                                        CUT TO:

80   EXT. BILL'S BOUTIQUE - DAY

PENNY is sauntering towards shop door. She takes
out key and looks idly along row of shop fronts.
Then freezes, surprised.

81   EXT. ANGLE ALONG PAVEMENT - PENNY'S P.O.V. - DAY

MIKE is crossing road and approaching door of his shop. He turns and obviously sees PENNY O.S. He stops and waves.

82   EXT. ANGLE ON MIKE'S SHOP - DAY

MIKE waits for PENNY, who comes along pavement towards him.

                    PENNY
          Coming home with the milk?

                    MIKE
          Never touch the stuff.

PENNY reaches him and they stand by door to Mike's shop.

                    PENNY
          Don't tell me you get up early to go to
          the market? Not in your line of
          business...though some of it's ripe
          enough for Covent Garden, I must say.

                    MIKE
           (jolted by an inexplicable echo)
          Covent Garden...

                    PENNY
          What's wrong?

                    MIKE
          Nothing.

                    PENNY
          You're not having one of your bouts in
          daylight now, are you?

                    MIKE
          I've just been out for a walk. Thought I'd
          savour the freshness of the air before
          other people got round to using it.

                    PENNY
          A likely story. You know you can't breathe
          until the atmosphere's at least 50 proof
          diesel fumes and cigarette smoke.

MIKE unlocks shop door and waves her in.

                    MIKE
          I'll offer you a cup of coffee before
          the day's work begins.

                    PENNY
               (glancing along street)
          I'm supposed to be in early. A whole
          lot of new stuff came in late last
          night and Bill asked me if I'd -

                    MIKE
          Blow Bill. Come and have coffee.

                    PENNY
          Well...if it won't take you too long to
          make it.

                    MIKE
          I was hoping you'd make it for us.

PENNY sighs and goes into the shop.

83 INT. MIKE'S SHOP - STOREROOM - DAY

     This is a small room at the back of the shop,
     crammed with bits and pieces. There is a

cluttered table under the window. MIKE hastily
tosses things off the table into an already
congested corner as PENNY comes to the table with
two cups of coffee. One item is a monstrous mug
with coloured pictures and lettering all over it.
MIKE inspects it with approval before putting it
aside.

                    PENNY
        What's that?

                    MIKE
        It's a mug.

                    PENNY
        Yes, but what's it for?

                    MIKE
        A thing of beauty is a thing of beauty
        in itself - it doesn't have to be for
        anything.

MIKE puts the mug down. PENNY puts the cups of
coffee on the table. They sit on rickety chairs,
wedged in among the chaos. MIKE lifts his cup to
his lips, and at once there is NOISE O.S. of
lorry discharging rubble.

                    MIKE
        Good God, have they started already?

MIKE looks towards the window.

84 EXT. DEMOLITION SITE - MIKE'S P.O.V. - DAY

A building is being pulled down; bulldozer
chucking broken bricks into a lorry, men setting
to work with picks on crumbling walls, etc. -

whatever shots are feasible. The ideal would be a
half-demolished house with one wall intact but
perilous, showing front door and a chimney which
still helps to hold the wall erect.

>MIKE (O.S.)
The only time we get any peace is
during the tea break - then there's
just a nice, soothing, slurping
sound.

85   INT. MIKE'S SHOP - STOREROOM - DAY

>PENNY
It's worse at our end of the street.
We're close to the bit where they're
burning all the old planks and things.

>MIKE
At lest you don't have to live on the
premises. I do. I get the lot.

>PENNY
Bill says the smell of smoke's getting
into the clothes on our racks. The
customers'll soon begin to notice.

>MIKE
Tell 'em it's all the rage. Make it a
selling point. Style with the Stench.
(looks out of window, upwards at an angle)
I'd love to get my hands on that grate
up there.

PENNY leans forward to see what he means.

(If possible insert:
85A.   LONG SHOT TEATERING WALL WITH A GRATE ON

WHAT USED TO BE UPPER STOREY.
If this is feasible, then some of ensuing
dialogue could be O.S. before cutting
back to Sc. 85

                    MIKE
On the third storey. Or what used to be
the third storey. I could get a good
price for that round here.

                    PENNY
But Chelsea's a smokeless zone.

                    MIKE
                 (pityingly)
I wasn't suggesting people should put
coal in it. Painted white and mauve
it'd make a marvellous rack for copies
of the Queen and Playboy.

RESUME GENERAL SCENE, angled on PENNY. She looks
around the room.

86 INT. MIKE'S SHOP - STOREROOM - PENNY'S P.O.V. - DAY

CAM PANS slowly as though inspecting the junk.
It stops on shelf, with large acid bottle
predominating.

                    PENNY (O.S.)
What's that?

                    MIKE (O.S)
Just what it looks like. A bottle of
acid.

87 INT. MIKE'S SHOP - STOREROOM - GENERAL VIEW - DAY

                    PENNY
I'll bet you're going to sell it at an
exorbitant price as a genuine old Roman
container for exotic spices.

                    MIKE
It's not for sale. I use it.

                    PENNY
What for?

                    MIKE
I knew you'd ask. For burning holes in
things to make them look authentic. And
sometimes to remove manufacturers names
from antiques.
                    PENNY
Why?

                    MIKE
Often the name isn't antique enough.

                    PENNY
              (getting up)
I must go.

                    MIKE
         (idly, not getting up)
What are you doing this weekend?

                    PENNY
Oh, I've got an awful lot of things to
do. I...well, I...

                    MIKE
I'm taking Saturday afternoon off. To
hell with BILL - come out with me. Into
the country.

                    PENNY
      Really, I ought to -

                    MIKE
      Ought! I <u>ought</u> to be off down the
      Portobello Road to see if I can pick
      up some old records of the Savoy
      Orpheans.

                    PENNY
      What for?

                    MIKE
      You can heat the records and make
      flower bowls out of them, the really
      'in' thing in S.W.3. I sell them
      by the score - or should I say by the
      78?

                    PENNY
      But why the Savoy Orpheans specially?

                    MIKE
      They seem to melt more easily. (A BEAT)
      Saturday, then?
                                        CUT TO:

88   EXT. COUNTRY ROAD - DAY

     LONG SHOT of undulating road. Motorbike in
     distance comes closer, travelling fast but not
     too madly.

89   EXT. TWO SHOT MIKE AND PENNY ON BIKE - DAY

     PENNY clings to MIKE, her head pressed against
     his back. She shouts in his ear but we cant hear
     her above the noise of the bike. She laughs.

90   EXT. COUNTRY ROAD - ANTOHER ANGLE - DAY

     MIKE and PENNY on bike, racing off into distance.

91   EXT. GRASSY VERGE OF ROADSIDE - DAY

     PENNY sprawled on grass, ravenously finishing a
     sandwich. MIKE bites into a plum.

91A CU MIKE

     MIKE is squashing the plum into his mouth. Juice
     runs down his cheeks.
                                              CUT TO:

91B INT. - MESMER'S ROOM - DAY

     MS MESMER drowning in wheelchair. He starts
     half awake, and a slow look of appreciation
     crosses his face. He wipes his mouth with his
     hand and licks his lips, sleepily tasting
     something.
                                              CUT TO:

91C EXT. GRASSY VERGE OF ROADSIDE - DAY

     MIKE lets himself sink back, his hands behind his
     head as he stares up at the sky.

                         PENNY
               A penny for them.

                         MIKE
               They're all about Penny.

                         PENNY
               Hm. Compliments yet.

                              PENNY
                          (probingly)
          The interest on this PENNY hasn't added
          up to much over the last year.

                              MIKE
             (stares up thoughtfully, then,
              abruptly sincere and troubled)
          Oh, love, why isn't it as easy for me
          as for other people?

                              PENNY
          If you'd only stop trying so hard and
          let yourself go - enjoy things a bit
          more.
                              MIKE
          Like Alan? All that earnestness. All
          that listening to music with such
          intensity...
                              PENNY
          What's wrong with really listening, if
          it gives you something extra?

                              MIKE
          Music's not for listening to. It's
          purely for drowning the yawns of
          frustrated humanity.

                              PENNY
          Oh, honestly...

          PENNY crumples up the paper in which the
          sandwiches were wrapped. MIKE rolls over on his
          side and stares vaguely at something O.S. Then he
          gets it in focus and begins to get up slowly.

                              MIKE
                      (still looking O.S.)

                               95

All right. Let's go and enjoy ourselves,
like you say. Wild abandon. The lot.

CUT TO:

91D. EXT - RIVER BANK - DAY

MIKE is in the shelter of the bank, slipping off
his jacket as he approaches the water. PENNY IS
on the bank above him, looking doubtful.

CUT TO:

91E EXT. RIVER - DAY

We are looking across the river. MIKE is swimming
naked, his clothes in a heap on the bank. PENNY
has come to the water's edge but is still
clothed.

                    MIKE
                 (taunting)
    What was that about letting yourself go?

PENNY defiantly puts hand up to blouse or dress
and begins to unbutton, loosen belt or whatever.

CUT TO:

91F EXT. RIVER - ANOTHER ANGLE - DAY

MIKE and PENNY swim closely together, laughing.
Play this for as long as required - perhaps
INSERTS of MIKE grabbing her wet shoulder as it
rises from the water, the two of them clinging
together, etc.

MIKE heads for a gnarled tree leaning out from
bank. He hauls himself partly out of water and
reaches out a hand to PENNY as she follows him.

91G EXT. RIVER BANK AND TREE - DAY

PENNY is lying on her face under the tree, with a
pattern of sunlight through branches on her naked
shoulder. MIKE is sitting beside her, looking
down as though trying to decide what he feels
about her. Slowly experimentally, he puts a hand
on her shoulder. PENNY stays quite still.

> (N.B This scene can be extended or
> developed if required, played for what
> it will carry - statement or implication.
> Perhaps use several closeups and
> angles within the basic scene.)

MIKE bends over PENNY and begins to grow
insistent. He tries to turn her towards him.
PENNY turns her head away and moans slightly,
resisting yet somehow being remorselessly turned
towards him. When he has got her halfway round,
MIKE pins down her head with a kiss, and his hand
moves O.S. down her body.

                    PENNY
        Mike...

PENNY jerks herself suddenly away and tries to
sit up, turned away from MIKE. She grazes the
tree and lets out a cry as her arm is slashed by
a branch.

                                        CUT TO:

91H CU PENNY'S ARM

There is a long, bleeding gash down her arm.
CAM PULLS BACK to take MIKE's head into shot as
he bends very slowly over the gash. There is
effect of slow motion here - of time suspended,

of MIKE descending very deliberately,
thoughtfully, towards PENNY'S arm.

                                    CUT TO:

92 INT. MESMER'S ROOM - DAY

MESMER, ESTELLLE and POKORNY are in different
parts of the room, but as we take up the scene
they are beginning to move slowly together into a
huddle as though craving warmth.

                    POKORNY
        Blood...he's not afraid of it.

                    ESTELLE
        He likes it !

                                    CUT TO:

93 EXT. GRASSY VERGE OF ROADSIDE - DAY
RESUME scene as in Sc.91 MIKE is dressed again,
but tousled. PENNY is shaking her wet hair. She
finds a button still undone and fastens it. She
glances uncertainly at MIKE.

                    MIKE
        Going to a concert with Alan tonight?
        Festival Hall...Albert Hall...?

                    PENNY
        I've have told you If I was. You know
        that.

MIKE stretches out on the grass.

                    MIKE
        No hurry to get back, then.

                                    CUT TO:

                      98

93A INT. MESMER'S ROOM - DAY

The three are in a close huddle, not yet in a
trance but beginning to concentrate hard.

                    MESMER
          He's a long way away.

                    ESTELLE
          But we want him back here. We've got
          work for him!
                    MESMER
          Yes, I think it's time he started on
          the homeward journey.
                                        CUT TO:

94 EXT. GRASSY VERGE OF ROADSIDE - DAY

MIKE and PENNY as we left them in Sc.93. Abruptly
MIKE looks at his watch and at once gets up.
PENNY blinks up at him, surprised.

                    MIKE
          It's clouding over. We ought to be
          getting back.

                    PENNY
          (shielding her eyes, looking into sky)
          Clouding over?

                    MIKE
          It'll be dark before we get to London.

                    PENNY
          Whoops. I'm not afraid of the dark.

                    MIKE
          No?

95   EXT. COUNTRY ROAD - TWILIGHT

TRACKING SHOT, wide angle, of bike racing along
road and over brow of hill.

96   EXT. TWO SHOT MIKE AND PENNY ON BIKE - TWILIGHT

Matching shot with Sc.89, but MIKE's expression
now is madly exultant and PENNY is scared
stiff.

PENNY
Mike...

97   EXT. COUNTRY ROAD - ANOTHER STRETCH - NIGHT

It is getting darker. The bike roars madly on and
screams round a corner.

98   EXT. DAZZLER OF ONCOMING LIGHTS - NIGHT
This will have to be tried ad lib - build up to
give jangling, dizzy, reeling blur.

CUT TO:

99   INT. THREE HEAD SHOT - NIGHT

Very quick shot, screen full of three heads -
MESMER, ESTELLE and POKORNY, lips parted,
grinning as they stare ahead, almost driving
the bike themselves. SOUND of bike O.S.
carries straight through from previous scene.
MESMER twists his head to look over his
shoulder into:

CUT TO:

100 CU PENNY

PENNY's face anguished, against blurred b.g.
Shifting lights dazzle across her face. We can
just hear her above the noise.

                    PENNY
          Mike....please....

SOUND of jumble of horns, other traffic, engine
noises. Through it, growing louder and then
drifting away, we hear ESTELLE cackling madly.
DISSOLVE PENNY into blur of light and then stop
dead as we
                                        CUT TO:

101 INT. MEMER'S ROOM - NIGHT

CU TABEL. POKORNY'S hand comes into frame and
places bottle on table. MIKE's hand moves in and
picks bottle up.

PULL BACK to take in MIKE, still tousled from the
ride. He puts bottle down, and goes out. We stay
on the door.

                  ESTELLE (O.S)
          And now...tonight we try?

                  POKORNY(O.S)
          The ultimate experience.

CAM PAN to take in MESMER from side angle. He
spins wheelchair to face us.

                    MESMER
The ultimate experience will be our own deaths.
I do not think we wish to indulge in that yet?

ESTELLE and POKORNY snigger dryly O.S.

                         MESMER
            Now...whom shall we choose?

                      ESTELLE (O.S)
            Anyone. Anyone at all.

                         MESMER
            Yes. At random. That will make it all
            grotesque.
                                                CUT TO:
102 EXT. STREET CORNER - NAME

     AUDREY and a girl FRIEND chatting on pavement,
     obviously about to separate.

                    MESMER'S VOICE (O.S.)
            At random.

     MOVES IN CLOSER to AUDREY and FRIEND.

                         AUDREY
            Well, see you tomorrow, then.

                         FRIEND
            And don't forget what I told you about
            that feller.

                         AUDREY
            You're not going to give me the chance,
            are you?

     Both girls laugh. FRIEND walks away.

                         FRIEND
            Goodnight, then.

                         AUDREY
            G'night.

AUDREY walks a few steps to door of nearby house.

103 EXT. SHADOWY DOORWAY - NIGHT

MIKE leans in doorway, face calm and reflective,
following progress of AUDREY O.S. He pushes
himself upright and walks unhurriedly out into
road.

104 INT. ANGLE UP A STAIRCASE IN SHABBY HOUSE - NIGHT

AUDREY is nearly at the top. When she has gone
round corner of landing, MIKE comes into shot and
starts to climb.

105 INT. BED-SITTER - NIGHT

AUDREY crosses room, puts down her handbag, and
slumps on to divan bed. She is reaching down to
take off her shoes when there is SOUND O.S. of
tap at door. AUDREY sits up and stares at door.

                    AUDREY
          Who is it?

SOUND O.S. of another tap at door. AUDREY
hesitates, then gets up and goes to the door. She
opens it. MIKE stands there, suave and polite.

                    MIKE
          Sorry to bother you, but you wouldn't
          happen to have a shilling?

                    AUDREY
          For the meter?

                    MIKE
          (insinuating himself a step into room)

I've just moved in upstairs and I can't
get the light on.

                    AUDREY
I know. You'll soon learn to build up a
little store.

AUDREY turns back into room and goes to shelf in
corner. It projects over end of divan, carrying
cutlery and oddments. She takes down an old
coffee tin, rattles it, and takes a couple of
shillings out.

                                        CUT TO:

106 CU MIKE

MIKE's expression changes from impassivity to a
taut, waiting savagery

                                        CUT TO:

107 CU MESMER

His face strained, willing something to happen.

                                        CUT TO:

108 INT. BED-SITTER - MS AUDREY - NIGHT

AUDREY turns with coins in outstretched hand. Her
helpful smile freezes and begins to fade. She
shuffles a step backwards.

MIKE moves into shot and blots out our vision of
AUDREY.

                    AUDREY
    No. I...no, don't...please...

MIKE's back darkens the whole screen.

109 INT. THREE-HEAD SHOT - NIGHT

MESMER, POKORNY and ESTELLE almost ghostly
against indeterminate b.g. Slowly MESMER raises
hand in slow, commanding gesture.

110 INT. BED-SITTER - ANGLE ON DIVAN - NIGHT

MIKE and AUDREY struggling madly on the bed. MIKE
is trying to strangle her.
(N.B - It would be worth shooting a lot of
footage on this, taking it as far as it will go,
but allowing for a dehydrated version for use in
the UK.)

MIKE suddenly repeats MESMER's gesture from
Sc109, carrying it through and groping up into
the air. His hand is near the shelf above the end
of the divan. MIKE had to let go of AUDREY for a
moment in order to kneel on the divan and reach
the shelf.

111 CU MIKE'S HAND AT SHELF

A breadknife is by his hand. The hand takes it.

112 INT. BED-SITTER - ANOTHER ANGLE - NIGHT

AUDREY flounders towards the door trying to
scream. She gets only a croak out. MIKE springs,
the knife held aloft. It descends and AUDREY goes
down. The knife stabs out of frame, again and
again. The scene DISSOLVES into a mad blur.

DISSOLVE TO:

113 EXT. BENCH IN SOHO SQUARE - DAY

If this is impractical, the bench could be a
studio shot against b.g. of a wall or a couple of
tombstones, implying some limited open space.

ESTELLE and POKORNY are on the bench. MESMER
drawn up beside the end of the bench in his
wheelchair. They look like three crumpled old
dears sunning themselves tranquilly while the
world goes by. MESMER has a newspaper on his lap.
He picks it up and nods contentedly over it.

                    MESMER
          Girl murdered in flat.

                    ESTELLE
               (leaning over his and reading)
          Sadistic killer at large.

                    MESMER
          They could hardly be expected to know it
          should be in plural.

                    POKORNY
          A very beautiful experience, I thought.

                    ESTELLE
               (nodding like a sweet old granny)
          Very beautiful.

                    POKORNY
          A dream no longer. Reality!

                    ESTELLE
          Real for us - not for him.

                    MESMER
          He wouldn't have appreciated it.

They all chuckle.

                    MESMER
         Such a lovely day! Think of all the
         things we can do - the things so many
         people would like to do but daren't.
                                          MIX TO:

114 INT. MESMER'S ROOM - NIGHT

         OUT TABLE. POKORNY'S hand comes into shot and
         puts bottle down. MIKE's hand takes it, as
         before.
                                          MIX TO:

115 EXT. BENCH IN SOHO SQUARE - DAY

         ESTELLE , MESMER and POKORNY exactly as in Sc. 113
         They have their eyes closed, basking.
         GIRL with transistor radio swinging from shoulder
         walks slowly past. Metallic voice speaks, and the
         three of them open their eyes and follow her
         progress drowsily, appreciatively.

                    RADIO VOICE (O.S)
         ...another vicious murder in the West
         End last night. The police believe that's
         the pattern of this killing and the one
         reported on...

         GIRL snaps switch over to pop programme. MUSIC
         crackles out O.S.

         ESTELLE, MESMER and POKORNY smile without looking
         at each other and close their eyes again like
         cats surfeited with cream.

         RADIO MUSIC O.S. carries over into:

116 INT. BASEMENT CLUB - ANGLE SINGLE/BAND - NIGHT

SINGER or BAND belting out as much as we need of
the number we have just heard on the radio.

117 INT. BASEMENT CLUB - ANGLE ON TABLE - NIGHT

LONG SHOT across club of MIKE, ALAN and PENNY at
table. They are talking casually. Then we see
MIKE glance at his watch and get up.

118 INT. BASEMENT CLUB - CLOSE ON TABLE - NIGHT

MIKE is on his feet. ALAN glances at PENNY.

                    ALAN
          Here we go again.

ALAN and PENNY also start to get up.
MIKE waves them down.

                    MIKE
          No need for you to come.

                    PENNY
          This time we want to join in the fun -
          whatever it is.

                    MIKE
          (glancing round contemptuously at room)
          Stay here and have your fun.

                    ALAN
          Mike - we want to know where you're going.

MIKE offensively ignores this and starts out
across the room. ALAN and PENNY silently consult
each other, then get up and follow.

119 EXT. STREET CORNER - NIGHT

(N.B - The following sequence of scenes should
build up tension - will they stop him, will they
track him down, will he get away...is something
going to crack? PENNY is scared, plays it all
flippantly but on the border of hysteria. ALAN
shows up as stubborn, serious , and basically
very strong and reliable.)

MIKE comes into shot on the corner and looks
round. ALAN and PENNY appear from shadows at his
elbow, from the opposite direction.

                    PENNY
                (too gaily)
        Fancy meeting you!

MIKE walks quickly down side street.
                                        CUT TO:

120 EXT. STREET OF CLUBS AND CAFES - NIGHT

MIKE crosses street at a diagonal. As he reaches
far pavement, ALAN and PENNY again appear and
intercept him. Play this in dumb show - seen from
a distance. PENNY pirouettes on the kerb,
pretending it's all a mad game.

                                        CUT TO:

121 EXT. STRETCH OF PAVEMENT - NIGHT

MIKE walks slowly towards us with ALAN on one
side and PENNY on the other. MIKE is silent,
looking straight ahead. PENNY tries to skip but
just looks clumsy.

                                        CUT TO:

122 EXT. STREET OF CLUBS AND CAFES - ANGLE ON
   DRINKING CLUB DOOR - NIGHT

There is nobody in the doorwa. CANNED MUSIC
jangles out form inside. MIKE comes into shot and
looks back, exasperated. ALAN and PENNY come into
shot and stop by him.

                    PENNY
        Excuse me - are we on the right road to
        Battersea Dog's Home?

                    MIKE
        Why don't you go home?

                    PENNY
        That's just what we want to do. We're a
        couple of strays, you see.

                    MIKE
        If you think this is some sort of game -

                    ALAN
        If it is, who started it? Mike.

                    MIKE
        Just go away. That's all. Go away.

RACHEL appears behind them in the doorway and looks
   out curiously

                    ALAN
        Won't you tell us what its all about?

                    MIKE
        Why won't you leave me alone?

                    RACHEL
        That's right, ducky. You tell 'em. Go
        on - why don't you let him alone?

ALAN puts a hand on MIKE's arm. MIKE shakes him
off.

                    PENNY
        Is this where you want to go Mike?
                (stares Rachel)
        Golly, it is the Dogs Home. Sort of.

                    RACHEL
        Come on, lover - you'll be all right in
        here. You know that don't you.

MIKE jerks away from them all and lunges across
the road. ALAN and PENNY doggedly go after him.

123 INT. MESMER'S ROOM - NIGHT

POKORNY is pacing to and fro. ESTELLE is at the
table, rapping her knuckles compulsively on it.
MESMER twists his wheelchair impatiently to and
from.

                    ESTELLE
        Concentrate, or we'll never get him
        here.
                    MESMER
                (fists clenched)
        He's got to come!

124 EXT. ANOTHER STREET CORNER - NIGHT

MIKE has turned at bay. ALAN and PENNY stop, and
he begins to harangue them.

                        111

                    MIKE
What good do you think this is going to
do?

                    PENNY
(wildly, talking for the sake of talking)
My horoscope today said I'd be going
for a long journey. Dead right. Haven't
walked so far since the last bus
strike.

                    MIKE
          (bitterly, to ALAN)
Call yourself a friend?

                    ALAN
          (very simply)
Yes.

                    MIKE
Why should I waste every minute of my
spare time with you?

ALAN stares gravely at him and doesn't reply.
This goads MIKE on.

                    MIKE
What do you expect to happen?

                    ALAN
I don't know. What do you expect to
happen?

                    MIKE
I...
     (falters, then it bursts out)
...for your own sakes, then...why waste
your time on me?

                     112

                    ALAN
        Friendship's not something you turn on
        and off like a tap, Mike.

There is a pause of absolute stillness. MIKE lets
himself sag against the wall.

                    MIKE
        Something's going to crack. Inside me.
                (put's hands to head)
        I'm being... used ...
                                        CUT TO:

125 INT. MESMER'S ROOM - NIGHT

MESMER slumps back in his wheelchair.

                    MESMER
        We can't shake them off. We must wait
        until tomorrow.

                    ESTELLE
        But the drugs? If we lose control of
        him tonight...
                    MESMER
        It won't lose its power entirely. We
        should still have enough contact to
        summon him for his repeat dose.

                    POKORNY
                (petulantly)
        But to have no pleasure tonight? All
        our plans...

                    MESMER
        Tomorrow.

                    POKORNY
        That friend of his - that impossible

young man - he's the one! We could have
shaken the girl off. But that young
fool...I'd like to settle with him.
            (looks from one to the other)
Our evening ruined...what can we do to
ruin something for <u>him</u>?

MIX TO:

126 INT. ALAN'S BED-SITTER - DAY

This is a small room with a lot of space taken
up by a grand piano. The place is in chaos.
Books and sheets of music torn up and scattered
all over the room. Snapped piano strings curl
out from under the piano lid. There are scorch
marks along the front of the piano and along
the keys.

ALAN, MIKE and PENNY are surveying it
incredulously.

                    PENNY
But who could have done such a thing?
Who'd have wanted...?

                    ALAN
                (wretchedly)
It make no sense.

                    MIKE
Someone seems to have it in for you.

                    ALAN
But who?
                    PENNY
            (stooping to inspect piano)
How did they do this - a hot poker, or
something?

                         ALAN
        Acid, I think.

                         PENNY
        Acid?

    PENNY turns, bewildered, to face:

126A INT. ALAN'S BED-SITTER - MS MIKE - DAY

    MIKE looks dazed, bewildered, but not guilty.

                         MIKE
        How did they get in?

    ALAN moves into shot and stands beside MIKE
    looking into the room as though trying to get a
    view that will make sense of the situation.

                         ALAN
        Oh, that wouldn't be difficult. Mrs
        Barnes is a trusting old soul - often
        leaves the door on the latch when she
        nips out shopping. I was in college,
        and the couple along the landing were
        out at work. It was easy enough - but
        why... why?
                                           CUT TO:

127 EXT. BENCH IN SOHO SQUARE (OR STUDIO ALTERNATIVE)
    - DAY

    POKORNY sits on bench with his hands folded
    across his stomach, his eyes shut, grinning
    complacently.
                                           CUT TO:

128 INT. STAIRCASE FROM ALAN'S FLAT - DAY

ALAN comes down with MIKE and PENNY behind him.
ALAN passes CAM. MIKE and PENNY come close into
shot and slow down. MIKE stumbles on the stairs,
looking down at his hands which he has opened out
before him.

                    PENNY
        What's the matter?

                    MIKE
        I don't know. I must have touched some
        of that mess in there. My hands
        feel...dirty. Dirty.

FADE on MIKE's puzzled, self-questioning face.

                                        FADE:

Perhaps we might go through a fade or a six, or
even a brief blackout, with three hammered guitar
chords which lead straight on into:
                                        FADE IN:

129 INT. BASEMENT CLUB - ANGLE ON STAGE - NIGHT
    Girl singer, LAURA, on stage. She sings a folk
    number or blues or whatever may be the current
    idion. The song should be an ironic commentary on
    certain aspects of the film - about, maybe, a
    'haunted' man who daren't look behind him because
    his memories are tracking him down. All very
    simple, naive ballad style, but with a double
    meaning.
                                        MIX TO:

130 INT. MESMER'S ROOM - NIGHT

    MUSIC continues O.S. through this scene but
    perhaps it's unsteady, rising and falling as

though coming in and out of the minds of the
deadly trio in gusts.

                  POKORNY
We must waste no time. He's got to be
called back. Now. The dosage must be
reinforced or we shall have lost him.

                  MESMER
It is still effective. I can feel the
chair he is sitting in. The table... And
I can hear the girl singing.

                  ESTELLE
His hands - his wonderful, strong hands!

The three of them bow their heads and
concentrate.
                           MIX TO:

131 INT. BASEMENT CLUB - ANGLE ON TABLE - NIGHT

If possible MIX so that the head of MESMER & CO.
give way gradually to heads of MIKE, ALAN and
PENNY, or match a CUT for similar effect.
LAURA is singing O.S.

Mike looks bored but not too irritable. ALAN and
PENNY are enjoying the song, but glance every now
and then at MIKE.

Abruptly MIKE gives a little start and glances
round as though someone had tapped him on the
shoulder. He starts to get up.

                  PENNY
Mike. You can't - not while while she's
in the middle of...

                    MIKE
        See you.

    MIKE is hemmed in by chairs and people, and makes
    a lot of noise as he tries to edge his way clear.

                    VOICES (O.S)
        Sash...Sit down.

132 INT. BASEMENT CLUB - ANGLE ON STAGE - NIGHT
LAURA singing.

133 INT. BASEMENT CLUB - ANGLE ON TABLE - NIGHT

    ALAN and PENNY have each grabbed on of MIKE's
    arms and are forcing him back into his seat.

                    MIKE
        I've got to go.

                    ALAN
        Wait till the number's finished.

                    MIKE
        I have no wish to wait till the
        number's finished.

                    PENNY
        You can't be in that much of a hurry.

                    MIKE
        I can't stand this row. That girl...
                (looks O.S. at stage)
        ...God, she's awful.

                    VOICE (O.S)
        Sash!

MIKE desperately tries to shake himself free.
ALAN won't let go.

                                          CUT TO:

134 INT. MESMER'S ROOM - NIGHT

MUSIC continues O.S. throughout.

The three are concentrating hard. Suddenly MESMER
sags and shakes his head.

                    MESMER
        It's no use. The tension could be
        damaging. Let him stay where he
        is...for the time being.

ESTELLE and POKORNY sit back, seething with rage.

                                          CUT TO:

135 INT. BASEMENT - ANGLE ON TABLE - NIGHT

MIKE sinks back into his chair. He looks dourly
at singer on stage O.S. He is resigned but bored.
ALAN AND PENNY exchange weary glances. Slowly
MIKE begins to frown.

                                          CUT TO:

136 INT. MESMER'S ROOM - NIGHT

                    ESTELLE
        He's beginning to hat that girl - the
        singer. Do you sense that?

                    POKORNY
        It's because of the struggle in his
        mind.

                        MESMER
    He is having to stay and listen to her
    when the impulses we have planted to
    him urge him to get away.

                        ESTELLE
    If only we could use that hatred!

MESMER drives wheelchair round room and swings it
so that he comes slowly at us, full face. We
settle on MESMER.

                        MESMER
    Until we have him completely under
    control again I think we should take no
    risks.

                    ESTELLE (O.S)
    But there's such a little risk.
                    (coaxingly)
    You can feel that we are still in close
    contact. It would be so...so delicious.

CAM PANS to take in ESTELLE, greedily
concentrating on MESMER.

                        ESTELLE
    I want that girl - that singer. So
    arrogant. And so young. She thinks that
    one day she'll be famous, with the
    world at her feet. Why should she? Why
    shouldn't she die tonight?

                        POKORNY
    If we could get him here first for a
    strengthening dose of the drug -

ESTELLE

She might have gone before we could get
him back to her. Or the anger would
have been dulled. Let's have him now,
and while he is in this mood!

MESMER

It would certainly add to the flavour.

POKORNY (O.S)

Can we resist it?

MESMER

No.

ESTELLE'S mad cackle blends with the music and
then drifts away, as the MUSIC carries us on to:

CUT TO:

136 INT. BASEMENT CLUB - ANGEL ON STAGE - NIGHT

LAURA finishes song. APPLAUSE O.S.

137 INT. BASEMENT CLUB - ANGEL ON TABLE - NIGHT

Across table we see LAURA in b.g. moving along
edge of room to a door. People congratulate her
as she goes.

MIKE slews round in his chair watching her. He
gets up without fuss. ALAN and PENNY look
apprehensive.

MIKE

Don't panic. I'll be back.
Sometime.

MIKE walks across room in directon LAURA has
taken. He is so casual about it that ALAN and
PENNY aren't sure how to react.

                    PENNY
        You think he's all right?

                    ALAN
        He'll have to be. Damn it, we can't
        follow him everywhere.

                    PENNY
        I can't. You can.

ALAN grins wryly and gets up. MUSIC starts up
again O.S and his way is blocked by dancers for a
moment or two.

138 INT. BASEMENT CLUB - CORRIDOR - NIGHT

A badly-lit corridor wit a door at far end,
half-open into street. Halfway along MIKE and
LAURA are chatting. We don't hear them at
this stage apart from a faint buzz of
conversation, but we hear LAURA laugh as
though MIKE has said something half outrageous,
half flattering.

ALAN comes into shot from behind CAM and stops so
that we are looking over his shoulder along the
corridor.

MIKE glances along corridor and sees him. He
raises a mocking eyebrow and deliberately turns
his back.

139 INT. BASEMENT CLUB - CORRIDOR - TWO SHOT
    MIKE AND LAURA - NIGHT

MIKE is being insolent and charming, really
putting on his act.

                    MIKE
     ...but you can hardly expect to make any
     progress in a dump like this.

                    LAURA
     People here have been very nice to me.

                    MIKE
     You don't want audiences to be nice to
     you. You need them to be tough - to
     demand the best you can give.

                    LAURA
     I don't see why they shouldn't be
     polite, listen to you - give you a fair
     chance.

                    MIKE
     No. The kind of song you sing ought to
     stir them up. Better have tomatoes
     thrown at you than polite applause.
     Tomatoes...
          (he is puzzled by an echo)
                                        CUT TO:

140 EXT. CLOSE SHOT OF WHEELCHAIR - DAY

     Very fast memory of SC.51, wheel squashing
     tomato.
                                        CUT TO:

141 INT. GREENGROCER'S SHOP - MS MIKE - DAY
     Fast memory of Sc. 72 - boxes shattering.

                                        CUT TO:

142 INT. BASEMENT CLUB - CORRIDOR - TWO SHOT
MIKE AND LAURA, FAVOUIRNG MIKE - NIGHT

                    LAURA
          You sound as though you'd like people
          to throw tomatoes at me.

                    MIKE
               (vague, puzzled)
          I...I'd like to see you standing up to
          real challenge.
               (effort to recover)
          There's a terrific little club on the
          south bank where you have to be good to
          survive. Really good. That's where you
          find out if you've got a future.

                    LAURA
          I've never heard of any good places on
          the south bank.

                    MIKE
          You haven't lived. (A BEAT)
          Do you want to live?

143 INT. BASEMENT CLUB - ANGLE ON DOOR - NIGHT

          PENNY is standing by door wondering whether she
          ought to follow ALAN - wondering when he's going
          to come back. He appears suddenly in doorway.

                    PENNY
          Where is he? He hasn't got away?

                    ALAN
          You might say he's got a way...with
          him. He's chatting up the blues chick.

                    PENNY
          But he said he couldn't stand her.

                    ALAN
          Must be one of those love-hate
          relationships.

                    PENNY
          What shall we do?

                    ALAN
          I've had enough of this 'me and my
          shadow' lark. We'll stay here and enjoy
          ourselves without him.

          PENNY and ALAN stare gloomily into the room.

144 EXT. A MAIN ROAD NEAR WATERLOO - NIGHT

          A pretty dispiriting road - wide and bright,
          but nothing going on. A taxi draws up at the
          kerb and MIKE gets out. He gallantly helps
          LAURA out. LAURA looks dubiously around
          while MIKE pays the driver. The taxi drives
          off.
                    LAURA
          You're sure you know where we are?

                    MIKE
          Yes, I know where we are.

                    LAURA
          Where are we, then?

                    MIKE
          Where all the best people live.

                    LAURA
Nobody's doing much living that I can
see.
                    MIKE
They're all inside - waiting for you.
Shall we go?

MIKE crooks his arm and waits for her to take it
so that they can cross the road. LAURA hesitates,
viewing the bleak prospect with suspicion.

                    MIKE
Scared? Sooner go on being a second-
rater all of you life?

                    LAURA
Who says I'm second-rate?

                    MIKE
Anyone who doesn't face up to challenges
is second-rate. Anyone who doesn't take
life with both hands...

MIKE holds his hands out before him as though to
grasp the world and tear it apart.

                                        CUT TO:

145 INT. MESMER'S ROOM - NIGHT

MESMER is in his wheelchair with hands out in
the same gesture as MIKE's in Sc. 144. ESTELLE
and POKORNY are close to him, concentrating.

                    POKORNY
Can we hold him? There is still time to
let go - and no harm done.

                    ESTELLE
                 (terrifyingly)
      But we <u>want</u> harm done.

                                        CUT TO:

146 EXT. LANE LEADING TO RIVER - NIGHT

    This is a gloomy little turning somewhere along
    Bankside - deserted at this time of night, quiet
    and sinister.

    MIKE is arm and arm with LAURA, leading her along
    the shadowy pavement. She stops and jerks her arm
    free.
                    LAURA
         I don't like this.

                    MIKE
         It takes a connoisseur to appreciate it.

                    LAURA
         I'm going back.
           (looks around, lost and helpless)

    SOUND of a melancholy hooter from the river.

                    MIKE
         Call you a barge, lady?

                    LAURA
         I don't believe there's any club down
         here.

    MIKE stands quite calm and still, looking at her
    with a pleasant half-smile.

                    LAURA
         What are you staring at?

                              MIKE
                  You, of course. Who else?

                                                    CUT TO:

147 EXT. MS LAURA AGAINST RIVER B.G. - NIGHT

    This should be a hazy dream shot - LAURA
    beautifully dressed, b.g. possibly of north bank
    of Thames lit up. If b.g. is difficult, it can
    be out-of-focus b.p of river, shimmering, with
    rippling MUSIC O.S.

                           MIKE (O.S)
                  What else is there to see?

                                                    CUT TO:

148 EXT. MS LAURA AGAINST DARK LANE B.G. - NIGHT

    LAURA in exactly the same position as in SC.
    147 but as before, looking scared, and drab
    b.g. of lane, a wall, the wharf at the end of
    the lane.

                              LAURA
                  Why've you brought me her?

                           MIKE (O.S.)
                  So that you can sing for us.

                              LAURA
          US...?

                                                    CUT TO:

149 INT. MESMER'S ROOM - NIGHT

    A very fast insert (subliminal, even) of face of
    MESMER, ESTELLE AND POKORNY against a blank b.g.
    They stare gloatingly straight at CAM.

150 EXT. LANE LEADING TO RIVER - NIGHT

MIKE stands facing LAURA. From now on he spoke gently, almost coaxingly - but the effect is to frighten her more and more.

> MIKE
> Yes. Us. That's why you came. Now let's hear you.

> LAURA
> But the club...where...?
> When we get there...
> (shaky, eager, starting to babble)
> Let's get to the club and I'll sing.
> What do they have - a band, or a trio, or just a pianist, or...?

> MIKE
> Sing.

> LAURA
> But I can't. Not here. Not just like that.

> MIKE
> (moves forward a slow pace)
> Sing. I want to hear you again - in the right surroundings. Go on...sing!

LAURA looks desperately from side to side, but MIKE dominates the lane. There is no way out. LAURA begins quaveringly to sing a few lines of the song we have heard earlier.

> MIKE
> Is that the best you can do? I thought better of you.

151 CU LAURA

Her lips tremble as she forces the words out.

>   MIKE (O.S)
>   More spirit in it, girl - more fire!

LAURA stops. She is terrified, she just can't get
the words out.

CUT TO:

152 EXT. LANE LEADING TO RIVER - MS MIKE - NIGHT

MIKE begins to pace slowly forward. CAM PANS with
MIKE and takes LAURA into shot. LAURA backs away.

>   MIKE
>   (plaintively)
>   Sing.

LAURA opens her mouth and utters a croak.

MIKE pounces on her. His hands reach for her
throat and LAURA lets out a hideous gurgle. The
two of them go down to the ground.

153 EXT. TWO SHOT MIKE and LAURA - SHOOTING DOWN AT
AN ANGLE - NIGHT

>   MIKE
>   Is that the best you can do? You can't
>   sing any louder?

CUT TO:

154 INT. MESMER'S ROOM - CU ESTELLE - NIGHT

ESTELLE is gloating, staring straight at us,

urging the whole thing on.

CUT TO:

155 EXT. TWO SHOT MIKE AND LAURA IN LANE - NIGHT

Very close on the two of them. MIKE struggling
LAURA. She is hardly stirring now.

>   MIKE
> Why won't you sing when I ask you?
> You'll never make it - never be a star.
> Never...

LAURA moans once and then is still. CAM MOVES IN
on MIKE'S face. It is blank and cruel, the eyes
quite dead. Then he blinks and shakes his head.
Twists his head towards us so that he is in full
CU. Puts one hand shakily to his forehead.

CUT TO:

156 INT. MESMER'S ROOM - CU MESMER - NIGHT

MESMER, staring straight ahead, begins to shake.
He looks alarmed.

>   MESMER
> He's drifting away from us.

>   ESTELLE (O.S)
> I can't feel...I can't see...

CAM PULLS BACK to take in ESTELLE and POKORNY.

>   POKORNY
> The drug has weakened.

>   MESMER
> We ought never to have risked it.

                    ESTELLE
                   (moaning)
        He's going...
                    MESMER
        Hold him - we must hold him!
                                           CUT TO:

157 EXT. LANE LEADING TO RIVER - NIGHT

        LAURA is a crumpled heap in the road. MIKE stares
        down at her, incredulous. He holds his hands out
        in front of him and stares at them. He whispers;
        then turns and runs madly away. CAM turns to
        follow him as he stumbles on into the shadows.

                                           SLOW FADE

                                           FADE IN:

158 INT. SNACK BAR - DAY

        PENNY is on high stool at counter. On the other
        side of the counter is OWNER, scuttling to an
        fro, serving customers. PENNY hums to herself,
        swings her legs, finishes a roll and cheese, and
        peers into glass case of other rolls and
        sandwiches, pulling weird faces as she does so.
        OWNER comes back along the counter and watches
        her, wondering if she is going to choose
        something.

                    OWNER
        Cheese and pickle?

        PENNY shakes her head.

                    Ham?

        PENNY shakes her head.

Liver sausage and gherking?

PENNY, with a slight wince, shakes her head.

Aren't you hungry?

                    PENNY
I want to lose a few inches.

                    OWNER
          (heavy-handed humour)
Vertically or horizontally?

PENNY grimaces.

                    OWNER
          (pressing it)
I mean, depends on whether skirts get
shorter or narrower, doesn't it?

PENNY looks round and smiles a greeting O.S.

ALAN comes into shot carrying an evening paper.
He climbs on stool beside PENNY.

                    OWNER
Cheese and pickles...ham...liver
sausage and gherkin?

                    ALAN
Nothing, thanks.

                    OWNER
This isn't a bus shelter, you know.

                    CUSTOMER
          (along counter)
Two espressos, please.

OWNER bustles away to serve him.

                    PENNY
        (smile dying as she looks into ALAN'S face)
            What's wrong?

ALAN mutely holds out the paper. PENNY takes it.

(If possible, insert: 158A CU PHOTOGRAPH LAURA ON
FRONT PAGE, WITH HEADLINE: BLUES SINGER SLAIN
Then resume 158 or, if not practicable to use
158A, go straight on anyway)

PENNY reads front page story with growing horror.

                    PENNY
            But this is the girl...Alan, he
            couldn't have! Not Mike!

                    ALAN
            I've been trying to work out whether
            those evenings he acted funny tie in
            with...
                (looks round, lowers voice)
            ...these recent murders.

                    PENNY
            And do they?

                    ALAN
            Too closely for comfort.

                    PENNY
            It must be coincidence. ALAN, it's got
            to be.

                    ALAN
            I think we'd better go and see him.

ALAN and PENNY slide from their stools and turn
towards the door.

                    OWNER
          (dashing along behind counterO
          And it's not a free soup kitchen,
          either.

PENNY fumbles in her bag and spills coins on the
counter. She hurries away without waiting for the
money to be checked.

                    OWNER
                (calling after them)
          Do come again.

159 EXT. MIKE'S SHOP - ANGLE ON DOOR - DAY

There is a 'CLOSED' notice dangling in glass
door. ALAN and PENNY approach and go up to door.

(Possibly insert:
159A CU NOTICE: CLOSED EVEN FOR THE SALE OF
ANTIMACASSARS)

ALAN presses bell push. O.S. SOUND OF BELL inside
shop. Nobody comes. ALAN glances at PENNY and
presses again. PENNY goes up to glass and presses
her nose against it. Turns back to ALAN. They are
both worried.

                    PENNY
          He must be...out buying something.
          New stock. Or something.

                    ALAN
          I hope so.

                        PENNY
        He...he'd hardly met her before last
        night, had he?

                        ALAN
        How should I know? I'm beginning to
        wonder if we've ever really known
        anything about him.

    PENNY tries pressing the bell, jabbing it several
    times to produce a clamorous signal.

                                            CUT TO:

160 INT. MIKE'S SHOP - STOREROOM - DAY

    MIKE is sitting on the floor, huddled against the
    wall below the window. His eyes move slightly as
    the SOUND OF BELL, loud in here, stabs through
    the shop. But then he resumes his contemplation
    of infinity.
                                            CUT TO:

161 EXT. MIKE'S SHOP - ANGLE ACROSS STREET - DAY

    PENNY and ALAN turn away and walk disconsolately
    away along the street.
                                            CUT TO:

162 INT. MIKE'S SHOP - STOREROOM - DAY

    MIKE'S lips move but for a moment nothing comes
    out.

    SOUND O.S. of demolition site activities - sudden
    roar of a lorry discharging rubble, or some such
    noise. MIKE seems to hear it from far away, and
    shakes his head. SOUND CEASES. MIKE produces a

whisper, as though in a trance.

> MIKE
> Where are you? You...where are you?

Suddenly he and we are hit by SOUND O.S. of
TELEPHONE RINGING in shop. MIKE twists round to
look at connecting door. His mouth trembles. At
last he pushes himself up and lurches towards the
shop.

163 INT. MIKE'S SHOP - ANGLE ACROSS COUNTER - DAY

We can either make this a fresh set-up, seen from
body of shop, or track with MIKE through
connecting door and stop with him as he stops
close to the telephone. He seems to be waiting
for it to stop ringing. But it won't. MIKE
reaches out waveringly and picks it up. He puts
receiver to his ear but can't utter a word.

164 CU MESMER AT TELEPHONE - DAY

MESMER is brooding lovingly over the phone. He
enjoys the silence at the other end.

> MESMER
> You seem to have got yourself into a
> spot of trouble.

> CUT TO:

165 INT. MIKE'S SHOP - MIKE AT TELEPHONE -DAY

MIKE stands rigid, hardly breathing. He still
can't speak.

> CUT TO:

166 CU MESMER AT TELEPHONE - DAY

                    MESMER
    You musn't be upset. If only you'd been
    a bit more obedient about your medicine,
    you need never known. But don't do
    anything rash. Between us we can
    straighten everything out.
                                    CUT TO:

167 INT. MIKE'S SHOP - MIKE AT TELELPHONE - DAY

                    MIKE
    Why me? Why did you pick on me?

    MIKE holds out his free hand and stares at it as
    though full memory is only just returning.

                    MESMER
                (O.S. filter)
    You must come to us. If you want to
    free yourself from your distress -

    MIKE bursts out suddenly.

                    MIKE
    What have you made me do? No, I wont
    come to you. Never again. Do you hear
    me?

                    MESMER
                (O.S. filter)
    I hear you. If you don't come to us. I
    think we shall have to come to you.

                    MIKE
    Don't try it. Stay away from me - do
    you get that? Stay away!

    MIKE slams down receiver and rocks to and fro for

a moment. Then he turns and lurches back towards
the storeroom.

168 INT. MIKE'S SHOP - STOREROOM - DAY

MIKE totters in and collapses against the wall.
O.S. SOUND OF TELEPHONES RINGING again. MIKE lets
it ring. Stares ahead.

>   MIKE
>   (whisper)
> Stay away.

At least TELEPHONE SOUND CEASES. MIKE puts his
hands over his eyes, shuddering, then takes them
away again. He looks round the cluttered
storeroom with growing incredulity.

>   MIKE
>   (more intense whisper)
> Stay away...

                                         CUT TO:

169 INT. MIKE'S SHOP - STOREROOM - MIKE'S P.O.V. -
    DAY

Angles in this sequence should be as eccentric as
possible so that we share in MIKE'S dizziness.
Maybe the characters could be seen in one take,
scooped up as it were in one sweep by handheld
cam. Or it may be better to break up into short
cuts. Basis, anyway, is:

169A   GREENGROCER crouches on floor in corner,
back against some of MIKE'S junk, in exactly same
posture as in SC.70.

169B   RACHEL, with one elbow on a heap of junk,

mouths soundless invitation.

169C   AUDREY is crumpled lifeless on the floor.

169D   RACHEL begins to dance round the room in
a hideous travesty of romantic sense in Sc. 44.
She reels closer to us, moving faster and faster.

> MIKE(O.S)
> Stay away.

The scene whirls and RACHEL collapses across
frame into:

169E - Heap on the floor which has been RACHEL
but whose distorted face we now see to be
LAURA'S.

CUT TO:

170 CU MIKE STARING

He is looking into this nightmare. Abruptly he
sees something else.

CUT TO:

171 INT. ALAN'S BED-SITTER - MIKE'S P.O.V. - DAY

The room in chaos just as we saw it in Sc. 126

> MIKE (O.S)
> My hands feel...dirty. Dirty.

CUT TO:

172 INT. MIKE'S SHOP - STOREROOM - DAY

MIKE leans against wall and looks round as though
daring the nightmare figures to reappear. He
blinks, tries to concentrate.

                              MIKE
        Alan...

He turns to connecting door and goes through into
shop.

173 INT. MIKE'S SHOP - DAY

MIKE lifts telephone receiver and dials.

                                            CUT TO:
174 INT. RECORD SHOP - DAY

ALAN at end of counter, already on telephone,
taking down orders on a piece of paper. SOUND of
records jingling through shop. CUSTOMERS in
booths. Mixture of several tunes all going
strong.

                                            CUT OUT:
175 INT. MIKE'S SHOP - DAY

MIKE with receiver to ear. We hear engaged tone.
MIKE presses rest down and dials again.

176 EXT. DEMOLITION SITE - HIGH ANGLE - DAY

Two figures - POKORNY and ESTELLE - scuttle along
edge of site. For next shot, zoom in if possible.
If not, straight cut to:

177 EXT. DEMOLITION SITE - GROUND LEVEL - DAY

POKORNY and ESTELLE stumble grotesquely over the
rubble like two creatures liberated from the
cellars of the dying building.

178 EXT. A STRETCH OF PAVEMENT - DAY

MESMER trundles along in his wheelchair at a
good, determined pace - obviously clear about his
destination and remorseless in his progress.

179 INT. BILL'S BOUTIQUE - DAY

PENNY is at telephone in middle of a
conversation. From time to time she glances
nervously at BILL, who is prancing about,
tweaking skirts and jackets, never content to
let well alone.

                    PENNY
          Of course we'll come. But can't you
          tell me anything now? All right. I'll
          get in touch with Alan. Somehow. I'll
          keep trying.
          Er...
               (glances meaningly at BILL)
          ...well, it's a bit difficult just now.

BILL gets the hint and makes a move.

                    BILL
          You can't say anything that'll shock me,
          dear.

                    PENNY
                  (into phone)
          It was you, wasn't it? I mean -
          well, you know.

                    BILL
          Oh, very well. Very well. If it's that
          complex...

BILL flounces through door into back of shop.

                         PENNY
          Yes. Bill was here, but he's gone into
          the back for a minute.
          We close in half an hour...No, I can't
          very well. But as soon as we've
          closed...
                      (puzzled)
          Who'll be coming for you? The police,
          you mean?...Who, then?
                                              CUT TO:
180 INT. MIKE'S SHOP - DAY

    MIKE at telephone, finishing conversation.

                         MIKE
          I'll tell you the lot when you get
          here. But - make it soon!

    He replaces receiver and glances idly towards the
    door.
                                        SHOCK CUT TO:

181 INT. MIKE'S SHOP - ANGLE ON DOOR - DAY

    MIKE'S P.O.V. on glass-panelled main door - and
    if possible we ZOOM IN across shop to near CU of
    MESMER, leaning forward in his wheelchair so that
    his nose is almost pressed to the glass. He taps
    the glass with fingernails and indicates that
    MIKE should let him in.

182 INT. MIKE'S SHOP - STOREROOM - DAY

    MIKE backs away towards door into storeroom.

183 INT. MIKE'S SHOP - STOREROOM - DAY

    MIKE comes in and looks desperately round. Picks

up and old pair of fire tongs for use as a weapon
and takes a step back towards connecting door.
Then his nerve fails him and he whispers. Drops
tongs and turns in panic towards back door.

(N.B. Layout of this scene will depend on
possible exits available to the demolition
site. Maybe the back door opens straight on to
the site or maybe there is an alleyway between
backs of the row of shops and the site. For the
time being I am assuming that the door opens
straight out on to at any rate a flat surface
close to the edge of the site and with ready
access to it.)

The inside of the back door is obscured by piles
of junk and obviously the door hasn't been used
for ages. MIKE claws stuff out of the way,
throwing boxes and bits everywhere. Clears the
door and fumbles with the bolts.

184 EXT. BACK DOOR OF SHOP - DAY

We are close on this door as it opens form the
inside and MIKE reels into the doorway. He holds
on to jamb for a moment and then lurches out into
the open.

CAM PULLS BACK fast to take in ESTELLE and
POKORNY, one on each side of door. They at once
close in on MIKE, ESTELLE'S clothes flapping
about her like a witch's tattered cloak. She
shrieks as she leaps. By sheer weight ESTELLE and
POKORNY carry MIKE back into the storeroom.

185 INT. MIKE'S SHOP - STOREROOM - DAY

MIKE, ESTELLE and POKORNY in a tangle of limbs,

crashing into the middle of the chaos. MIKE
lashes out and sends POKORNY staggering. ESTELLE
sees the tongs and grabs them. She strikes MIKE
across the back of the head and he goes down,
dead to the world. POKORNY leans against the
wall, panting.

> POKORNY
> Oh, dear. We're not used to such
> exertion. Bad for us.

> ESTELLE
> I prefer my violence secondhand.

They both chuckle breathlessly. ESTELLE turns
towards the connecting door.

186 INT. MIKE'S SHOP - ANGLE ON DOOR - DAY

MESMER is waiting outside in his wheelchair.
ESTELLE crosses the shop, opens the door. MESMER
wheels himself in and heads straight for
connecting door.

187 INT. MIKE'S SHOP - STOREROOM - DAY

MESMER wheels in through the door and looks down
with satisfaction at MIKE. He nods to POKORNY,
who lifts MIKE up into sitting position. MESMER
reaches down behind him into a pocket in the
wheelchair and takes out a bottle. He hands it to
POKORNY, who stops over MIKE and begins to force
his lips apart.

ESTELLE edges towards MIKE and strokes his head
with an awful sexy-maternal devotion.

188 INT. BILL'S BOUTIQUE - DAY

PENNY is at telephone, just finishing dialling.
BILL comes back into shop from back room and
looks at her in dismay.

> PENNY
> (into phone)
> Alan? Oh, thank heavens. Look, can you
> get away early tonight? Yes, I know
> it's one of your late days, but you've
> got to. Because of...

BILL turns wearily towards the back room.

> BILL
> Really, the complexity of our love life!
> Abstinence would be so much simler.
> (reaches door, and adds before disappearing)
> And so much better for the telephone
> bill.

BILL leaves room.

> PENNY
> (into phone)
> Just as soon as you <u>can</u>, then.

189 INT. MIKE'S SHOP - STOREROOM - DAY

MIKE, still propped up, opens his eyes. MESMER
and the other two form a little arc hemming him
in. MIKE gets them in focus and begins to push
himself up.

> MIKE
> You...What are you doing here?

> MESMER
> You needed our help, so we came.

MIKE

I don't need you. I don't want anything
more to do with you.

ESTELLE

Oh, you do, my dear. Really you do.

MIKE

Get out. The three of you - go on. I'm
not going to submit again. I'm not
going to...

MIKE'S voice falters. He stares as POKORNY
quietly and significantly up-ends the small
bottle to demonstrate that it's empty.
POKORNY then puts it on the table under the
window.

MESMER

There are so many pleasures still in
store for all of us.

MIKE

You can't go on using me like that.
People will guess about last night. My
friends will. The police are bound to
get on to it before long.

MESMER

On to you, possibly.

MIKE

If I'm caught - if anything happens to
me...

MESMER

We shall have good warning. Enough time
to withdraw. Whatever's in your mind, we
shall know it. You can't take us by
surprise unless you take yourself by

surface - and how do you that?

MIKE is on his feet. He turns towards the back door. They let him reach it, and then MESMER, ESTELLE and POKORNY concentrate...and MIKE is at a standstill.

190 INT. MIKE'S SHOP - STOREROOM - ANGLE ON MIKE - DAY

MIKE is in f.g. with the other three in a huddle behind him. MIKE'S face twists as he tries to move.

> MESMER
> It will be better for you to accept us. Do what we say, and there may still be hope for you.

> MIKE
> (grinding the words out)
> Hope - or whay? Of more killing? I won't go on. You can't make me go on.

CAM moves past MIKE and closes in on MESMER, POKORNY and ESTELLE. They leave MIKE where he is, petrified, discussing him as though he weren't there.

> POKORNY
> In his mind I read that he has been talking to that girl. She is coming here -and perhaps bringing the other. That meddling young fool.

> MESMER
> So much the better.

                    ESTELLE
          He mustn't talk to them.

                    MESMER
          But yes. Let him talk. Let us suffer
          his remorse.

                    ESTELLE
          Ah! Yes...yes. I'd rather like to
          experience the sensation of remorse. It
          will be a new flavour.

                    POKORNY
          But if he tells everything -

                    MESMER
          They're unlikely to believe. And in any
          case...they won't live to tell the
          story to anyone else.

MIKE makes a tremendous effort and, while they
have let their concentration lapse during this
discussion, forces his way towards the connecting
door.
                    MIKE
          I'll...stop them coming.

They concentrate now, and stop him once more.

                    MESMER
          No, You won't stop them. You'll let
          them come. And then you will dispose of
          them. When we tell you.

191 INT. BILL'S BOUTIQUE - DAY

          PENNY is tidying up shop. She glances at her
          watch as BILL comes in from the back room.

                              BILL
          It's too bad. At this time of day they
          really ought to damp that fire down. It
          was just that sort of thing that
          started the Fire of London. I wonder if
          one of us ought to stay on to make sure
          the place is safe...?

PENNY looks at her watch again - this time very
markedly, glaring at it.

192 INT. RECORD SHOP - DAY

ALAN has just dealt with a CUSTOMER who is going
out. He turns to HARRY? Sorry, but it is rather
special.

                              HARRY
          Sure. But try to clear those two over
          there before you go, will you?

They turn to look at two booths where GIRL A and
GIRL B are swaying to and fro in completely
different rhythms. GIRL B is ecstatic, shaking
everything that will shake.

193 EXT. BILL'S BOUTIQUE - DAY

PENNY comes out and closes door behind her. She
hurries away along the pavement.

194 INT. RECORD SHOP - DAY

ALAN, exasperated, stares at the two girls, still
listening and quite unconscious of his attempt to
will them out of the place. GIRL B is really on a
cloud.

195 INT. MESMER'S ROOM - DAY

The door opens and MESMER leads the way in.
POKORNY and ESTELLE drag chairs forward so that
they can form a close huddle.

> MESMER
> Now. Let's see how things are
> progressing, shall we?

They lower their heads in concentration.

196 INT. MIKE'S SHOP - DAY

PENNY and MIKE are in a corner of the shop,
hidden from the window by a gimmicky erection of
the stock in trade. The more incongruous the
setting and the angle, the better. PENNY and MIKE
have been talking earnestly against a backdrop of
gaudy, frivolous fantasy.

> PENNY
> So it wasn't just last night. You're
> sure about the others as well?

> MIKE
> Quite sure.

> PENNY
> But you didn't leave any clues. No-one
> suspects you.

> MIKE
> And that makes it all right?

> PENNY
> I didn't say it made it all right. Just
> that...

                    MIKE
Well?

                    PENNY
It gives us time to think.

                    MIKE
I don't know that I want to think. More
than anything in the world I'd like to
be able to stop thinking. Stop
remembering.

                    PENNY
But somehow we've got to work it out.
Before anyone gets on to you - if they
ever do...

                    MIKE
There'll be other people at the club
who saw me with Laura. That was her
name, wasn't it?

                    PENNY
You're not even sure about that? In
spite of what... of what...

                    MIKE
Of what I did? What I did...Only it
wasn't really me.

                    PENNY
You mean it was - well, you weren't
yourself at the time?

                    MIKE
I was three other people. Three old,
terrible creatures. They used me. Three
of them...

PENNY feels he is mad. She tries to look
sympathetic and understanding, but she doesn't
know what is going on.

197 INT. RECORD SHOP - DAY

ALAN is impatiently sliding a record into a paper
carrier and changing a £5-note for GIRL A from
Sc. 192/1XX. As he finishes and GIRL A leaves,
GIRL B saunters back from booth she was in. GIRL
B has, right till the last second, been quivering
ecstatically.

                    ALAN
        You like it?

                    GIRL B
                (deadpan, languid)
        No.

GIRL B walks out. ALAN watches her go and then
shrugs resignedly at HARRY.

                    ALAN
        Well, if it's all right with you -

                    HARRY
        Sure. See you tomorrow.

ALAN takes jacket from peg behind counter.

198 INT. MIKE'S SHOP - DAY

PENNY is half turned away from MIKE, trying to
sound very rational and detached - and sounding
in fact very edgey.

                    PENNY
        MIKE, don't you think - before things

get any worse - you ought to see
someone about all this?

> MIKE
>
> I'm seeing you. Would you sooner I
> nipped along to Scotland Yard?

> PENNY
>
> No, I mean...this business of the three
> other.

> MIKE
>
> You don't believe in them?

> PENNY
>
> Well...I believe that you believe in
> them. I'm sure if you could talk it
> over with a doctor - I mean. I know
> people get these ideas...and they must
> be very real...

> MIKE
>
> Schizophrenia, hm? Very useful. Only
> most schizos make do with a split down
> the middle. Typical of your old friend
> Mike, isn't it? - he has to have three
> others round his neck.

199 EXT. KING'S ROAD - CHELSEA - DAY

ALAN in rickety old car is trying to drive out of
a side turning into King's Road. There is a
traffic snarl-up. ALAN fidgets, leans out,
mutters curses to himself and others.

200 INT. MIKE'S SHOP - DAY

MIKE and PENNY are in same position as in Sc. 198.

                    PENNY
Look, MIKE. Three others or not - you,
or something outside you, or...oh, I
don't know...whatever it is, how do you
know it won't happen again?

                    MIKE
I don't.
                    PENNY
You've no idea _when_ it might happen?
You don't get any warning? - who it
might be, or when, or...it could be
anytime at all...anywhere?
                                        CUT TO:

201 INT. MESMER'S ROOM - DAY

The room is gloomy as twilight begins to settle
down, MESMER, ESTELLE and POKORNY are grouped
together.

                    MESMER
I think we might take her up on that.

                    ESTELLE
She _is_ asking for it, isn't she?

                    MESMER
Let us indulge ourselves. Now...

202 INT. MIKE'S SHOP - DAY

MIKE stiffens. He has been on the defensive so
far, but now savagery starts to take over.

                    MIKE
You don't believe a word I've told you,
do you?

                     155

                    PENNY
        It's all a bit difficult to understand.
        At first, that is.

                    MIKE
        Perhaps I can help you to understand.

MIKE moves towards PENNY. PENNY steps back and
looks round. It dawns on her that she is in
peril. So far it has been an academic discussion.
Now she is face to face with a potential killer.

                    PENNY
                 (placatingly)
        Mike, we've got to talk this out
        reasonably.

                    MIKE
        Reasonably?

MIKE advances. PENNY dodges and tries to get
round the end of the counter. MIKE intercepts her
and suddenly, with terrifying unexpectedness,
takes her arm and twists her violently so that
she is thrown into a corner at the back of the
shop.

                    PENNY
        MIKE - you've got to listen!

                    MIKE
        You talk too much. I'll have to stop
        that.
                                        CUT TO:

203 INT. MESMER'S ROOM - DAY

        CLOSE on faces of MESMER, ESTELLE and POKORNY.

                        156

They are silent, engrossed - living every moment
to the full.

CUT TO:

204 INT. MIKE'S SHOP - DAY

MIKE and PENNY are fighting madly in a corner. We
are right in the middle of it with them. They
blunder through a grotesque fantasia of the
shop's gimmicks - grabbing them, fighting with
them, a hideously comic no-holds-barred scrimmage
with every ludicrous bit of junk that comes to
hand. PENNY raises one hand and slashes her nails
down MIKE's face.

CUT TO:

205 INT. MESMER'S ROOM - DAY

CU POKORNY. He raises his hand smartly to his
cheek and gasps, reacting to the pain.

CUT TO:

206 INT. MIKE'S SHOP - STOREROOM - DAY

MIKE and PENNY, locked in battle, stagger through
the doorway and crash into the litter of junk
still lying about the place. The fight goes on ad
lib as long as it can be sustained.

207 INT. MIKE'S SHOP - ANGLE ON DOOR - DAY

ALAN rushes up to door from outside. He seizes
handle and rattles it, peering in.

208 INT. MIKE'S SHOP - STOREROOM - DAY

PENNY breaks free from MIKE and dashes through
connecting door to shop.

209 INT. MIKE'S SHOP - ANGLE ON DOOR ACROSS SHOP -
DAY

PENNY races across our line of vision. As she
clears, we see ALAN smash glass and put his hand
in to unlock door. Immediately ROUND O.S. of
burglar alarm above shop door.

> PENNY
>
> Alan!

MIKE dashes into centre of shop and makes a grab
for PENNY. She dodges, and next moment ALAN is
beside her. They face MIKE. ALAN advances slowly
on MIKE.

> ALAN
>
> Take it easy, Mike. What -

MIKE grabs a large ornamental wastepaper basket
and hurls it at ALAN. ALAN goes backwards into
the stuff in the window. MIKE turns and runs back
into the storeroom.

210 INT. MESMER'S ROOM - DAY
The three look grimly ahead and talk without
relaxing their concentration.

> POKORNY
>
> We must let go.

> MESMER
>
> No! He must be helped to escape. We
> don't want to leave him now!

> ESTELLE
>
> I can't do without him now!

                    MESMER
              (straight ahead)
        Move!

                                              CUT TO:

211 INT. MIKE'S SHOP - STOREROOM - DAY

    MIKE blunders towards back door and wrenches it
    open as ALAN comes through connecting doorway
    from shop.

212 EXT. DEMOLITION SITE - DAY (PERHAPS TWILIGHT)

    MIKE runs across rubble, trips, and falls on one
    knee.

                                              CUT TO:

213 INT. MESMER'S ROOM - DAY (TWILIGHT)

    CLOSE on three heads: ESTELLE, POKORNY and MESMER
    all wince and flinch in unison.

214 EXT. DEMOLITION SITE - DAY

    LONG SHOT of MIKE running, with ALAN close
    behind.
215 EXT. DEMOLITION SITE - ANOTHER ANGLE - DAY

    FIRST WORKMAN AND SECOND WORKMAN getting ready to
    knock off. FIRST WORKMAN offers SECOND WORKMAN a
    cigarette.

                    FIRST WORKMAN
          Feel like a pint, Bert? Get the dust
          out of your throat.

                    SECOND WORKMAN
                     (coughing)

A pint on top o' this'd make smashing
porridge.

They turn to walk off, when FIRST WORKMAN spots
something.

                    FIRST WORKMAN
          Hey - what the hell do they think
          they're playing at?

216 EXT. DEMOLITION SITE - WORKMEN'S P.O.V - DAY

          MIKE running at an angle across site, weaving to
          shake ALAN off.

                    FIRST WORKMAN (O.S)
          Hey, you - where d'you think you're off to?

217 EXT. DEMOLITION SITE - PANORAMIC SHOT - DAY

          Take in as much as possible - ALAN after MIKE,
          TWO WORKMENT lumbering in at an angle to
          intercept MIKE.

218 EXT. DEMOLITION SITE - MS MIKE - DAY

          MIKE stops and looks from side to side. Then
          dashes off at another angle. He heads straight
          for the one remaining wall of the building,
          driven this way by the convergence of Alan and
          the two workmen O.S. CAM stays on MIKE as he goes
          towards steps leading up to front door of the
          solitary wall. ALAN and TWO WORKMEN come into
          shot, almost herding him.

219 EXT. DEMOLITION SITE - ANGLE ON DOOR IN WALL -
    DAY

MIKE reaches door and puts hand out to slam it
open.

220 EXT. DEMOLITION SITE - ANGLE ON FAR SIDE OF DOOR
 - DAY

This may in fact be better as studio shot. The
door is glimpsed briefly, bathed in flickering
red light. Door opens and MIKE reels forward -
his face becoming crimson in blaze of flame.

221 EXT. DEMOLITION SITE - SIDE ANGLE ON WALL - DAY

This should be angled to show the edge of the
wall and the fire blazing on one side. A dark
silhouette (dummy MIKE) falls from open doorway
into the flames, which billow up.

222 INT. MESMER'S ROOM - DAY

CLOSE on the three faces. A red light wipes
across them. Their mouths in agony.

                    POKORNY
        Let's go...!

ESTELLE screams. MESMER rasps incoherently in his
throat. They are engulfed by blaze.
                                        MIX TO:

223 EXT. DEMOLITION SITE - ANGLE ON FIRE - DAY

We MIX through from Sc.222 in a swirl of flame,
with faces of POKORNY, MESMER and ESTELLE
dissolving as gruesomely as possible into the
fire. CAM PULLS BACK to show that this is in fact
the fact below the half-demolished building. Dark
smouldering mass in centre of fire.

224 EXT. DEMOLITION SITES - ANGLE ON ALAN - DAY

ALAN turns away. TWO WORKERS back out of shot,
staring incredulously. PENNT, dishevelled, gropes
over rubble towards ALAN and stops by him. He
puts his arm round her shoulders.

                    PENNY
What...what drove him to it?

                    ALAN
We'll never know.

                    PENNY
He was going on about people using him
- three of them, making him do all
those things...

                    ALAN
Phantoms of his imagination.

                                    CUT TO:

225 INT. MEMSER'S ROOM - DAY

MESMER, POKORNY and ESTELLE lie twisted on the
floor. MESMER'S face predominated - turned
towards us, charred and hideous, the mouth open
as though screaming in a last agony.

As we slowly FADE, MUSIC of Laura's song builds
up ironically O.S.

THE SORCERERS HAPPENING

Extract from the book Michael Reeves *by Benjamin Halligan*

MIKE, NOW A SEMI-PROVEN QUANTITY, ARRIVED BACK IN London in early 1966 with the sole intention of netting an established production company for the next film. Like *Intrusion*, it would be a 'Leith Production'. He enlisted his Radley friend and *Intrusion* cameraman, Tom Baker as a generic 'assistant director' and drove him out to Kilburn to see *Revenge of the Blood Beast* for which Mike provided a running commentary. This was a common occurrence whenever Mike spotted the film playing. Tom, graduated from Trinity and working on shorts with Iain Sinclair, had been keeping an eye on Mike's progress and was keen to join in the fun. After *Carrion*, Tom had written a fanciful script for him, much in the manner of the European art cinema of the time; females as ciphers for aspects of the male protagonist, embodiments of different philosophies towards life. Here an artistic director ditches his 'straight' girlfriend for an older, bohemian woman and they elope with the straight girlfriend in pursuit; soul-searching, romantic ennui and canal-bank walks follow. But even then Mike was only interested in refining his abilities as an action director; some sequences were shot but *Tale of an Artist* remained unfinished.

Emboldened, Mike now forcibly introduced himself to a number of London film types and, so looking for trouble, encountered Michael Klinger of the Compton Group. Klinger already had a couple of ultra-cheap horror films under his belt, and from his vantage point on film-making, Mike would have been seen as a 'do-er' in a field, low-budget horror exploitation, that was eminently do-able. There was very little to lose, so Klinger made a token investment by packing Mike off to Rome, with Tom in tow, to develop the next film. The intention was that it would star Christopher Lee, utilising Mike's Maslansky connection. Offices were hired, a script of sorts was pieced together, 'research' into seventeenth-century costumes was underway, locations were scouted and a palace was examined. There would be a shot seen from across the palace gardens; Lee looming out from a window and glowering into the night. But things were slow. Mike would disappear off to see his girlfriend, who had a temporary position as a PA to Raquel Welch, then filming in Spain. Raquel's future husband, Patrick Curtis, was living in Rome and fell in with Mike and his friends at the Cowboy, a hamburger and rib joint part-owned by Patrick. Klinger arrived for a few days to see how things were progressing. By mid-1966, Mike had little more than talk, pitches, a useful trust fund to keep the spaghetti and Peroni flowing and a track record as film director consisting of *Revenge of the Blood Beast*. Lee passed and everyone decamped back to London.

Mike took up residence in a cottage in Knightsbridge, 23 Yeoman's Row. He stuck Hopper prints on the walls, placed a display hash pipe on the mantelpiece in the same way that, at the start of the decade, a prized copy of the Penguin Lady Chatterley's Lover would be deployed and installed a 16 mm projector in the untidy living room. He hired prints to watch with friends, read the film trade papers, read books that might make good films, prepared pitches and scripts (*Manic Mind*, *The Crooked Cross*, *Blood Moon*, retitled *Flame in the Blood*), all under the aegis of Leith Productions; despite the blow, Mike was determined to keep Leith Productions active. A strong script was needed rather than just persuasive talk. The opportunity arose when Mike chanced upon the writer Alfred Shaughnessy at a party. Shaughnessy had previously directed a number of potboilers and was now turning out film and television scripts to order ('"Some writers call this "whoring"...'). For Mike, Alfred was someone who could bring his extensive film production experience to scripting Mike's ideas, as well as providing advice and contacts, assist with the casting, and lend a professionalism to any proposed project. Mike hit him with the Siegel story, Alfred approved and liked Mike. His talent—'he could think in images'—was apparent even if, at present, there was little quality to show for it. The idea was psychological horror: a villa in the south of France, twin brothers, one a brilliant musician but quite insane, and a monstrous, Hitchcockian mother. It was called *Appassionata* and was to be a film under the sign of Roman Polanski, whose new film *Repulsion* showed just what could be done. Mike and Alfred thrashed out the *Appassionata* script over lunches (after one, Mike surprised Alfred with a print of his 1960 film *The Impersonator*). It would be pitched straight to Compton using the Klinger connection—and Compton made *Repulsion*. The film was constructed across modest lines, designed to be manageable within the confines of a low budget. The cast would include Christopher Lee, Flora Robson and Susan Hampshire. Compton made positive noises but the film was not to happen in this form.

At any rate, subtle psychological horror may have been Polanski's forte, but it was not at all Mike's beat nor, Polanski aside, was it really Compton's thing either. *Appassionata* was the second dead-end.

Patrick Curtis was a frequent guest at Yeoman's Row and someone thar Mike had now cast as a producer for an anticipated Leith Production. Patrick was an American film type (an actor and producer) then between Rome and London with Welch, the other half of his Curtwel Productions Inc., and was happy to join the gang for loud Monopoly games back at Mike's place when in London. Patrick found Mike 'effervescent about film' and so was keen to oversee the next film, which would even be ideal for Raquel, although the nature of the production would clearly be a few cuts below the type they were getting used to.

Robin Dalton, the literary agent, then making headway into London's artistic and aristocratic circles, introduced Mike to John Burke. John had been European Story Editor for Twentieth-Century Fox, earning money on the side by 'novelisations' of film and TV scripts. At some point when the latter became more profitable than the former, John went freelance and so the meeting with Mike was timely. He had sold an option on his 1965 treatment for *Terror for Kicks* which had since lapsed, and so the treatment was rapidly bought up by Leith Productions Limited of St Helier, Jersey, most probably with Mike's own money. John recalls that '[Mike wanted] a film produced fast because of some deal he was setting up'. It may have been an impulse buy as Mike seems to have gone soon cold on the idea—perhaps a horror action film featuring a young Mod mechanic seemed limited. Such details in the outline belong firmly to the identity-crisis interzone of British mid-1960s film production—northern realism out, and the swinging London wave was yet to occur. The resultant films often sported proles in the context of 'intelligent' entertainment (Reisz's *Night Must Fall*, for example). But John also had a treatment for a more intriguing proposition, *The Devil's Discord*, and an option was taken out on the 18 August 1966 and *Terror for Kicks* was shelved. John began working on *The Devil's Discord*, expanding it to feature-length abd adjusting the characters so that the film could accommodate Raquel, and a substantial role that would be offered to Christopher Lee.

The Devil's Discord was a solid haunted-house story. Havoc ensues when a lost piece of music, Sanducci's 'Satan's Sonata', is discovered. The locals are superstitious, experts are called in, a bloody history is seen in flashback:

Sanducci must have been working on some extraordinary harmonic theory. In writing music the way he did, he must have been aware of special resonances that can't be shown on paper. You know . . . a lot of the hysteria produced by so-called magic spells could be due to the musical content of the incantations. When witches and sorcerers claimed to call up devils, it wasn't the words that counted — most of them were gibberish anyway. What cast the spell — on the audience, if nobody else — was the musical rhythm amd melody. That's why so many of the words were nonsense: it's the overall sound that counts.

The music raises the dead love of the protagonist's eighteenth-century ancestor, Sanducci. There is unfinished business; she was executed over an affair with Sanducci and is now 'a creature from some cold hell'. It draws from the same mainstay of horror films that *Blood Beast* also tapped, with the breaking of past-present dichotomy. Had it been shot, the film might even have made *Blood Beast* seem like a dry-run. The final screenplay was complete by early October, but when 'casting complications' arose, Tigon decided to pass; this was the third dead-end. Classy horror featuring Christopher Lee was not working.

Something altogether different was needed, something with a few ambitions, and perhaps the answer came when Michael saw Compton's new film, *The Projected Man*: straight-up sci-fi horror, idea unashamedly ripped off from *The Fly*; scientists bark mumbo-jumbo at each other, experiment goes wrong, one of their number — a murderous mutant afizz with electricity — sets off on a killing spree around London by night. The film gingerly pushes the envelope in terms of nudity and innuendo. It was flat and formulaic, across a number of locations; the script seemed to have written itself. It opened in a handful of cinemas and few people cared less. This is what Compton could and did do—Mike had been wrong to worry about a strong script; what was needed was an outline intrinsically suited to a Compton film. He contacted John and requested rewrites on *Terror For Kicks*; the first thing that needed changing was the protagonist's profession and social class. Beyond that, the film must represent a framework for a highly contemporary London setting. And Polanski, who had unintentionally sent out the wrong signal with the success of *Repulsion*, was now about to unintentionally facilitate an opportunity for such a Compton-style project to get a green light; it was Polanski's scrambling, first out of Poland, then out of London, that allowed Mike to slip in.

Polanski's calling card was *Knife in the Water*. He had then attempted, unsuccessfully, to court Hammer with the script *If Katelbach Comes*. But Compton were prepared to bankroll his intentions for an English-language film, which was then to be called *Loveli Head*. While Mike was in Rome, Polanski arrived in London at the invite of Compton, hoping he could replace the drab Lodz soundstages with at least some of the trappings of Western wealth. Polanski recalls:

The Compton Group rejoiced in a high-sounding name, an elaborate letterhead, and a board of directors that included the Earl of Kimberley. Everything seemed to suggest that it was a major entertainment and communications conglomerate. Actually it owed its existence and main revenue to a small, seedy Soho establishment called the Compton Cinema Club, which showed what currently passed in London for porno movies... The Compton Group had been making so much money out of this operation that it was anxious to change its name...

Low-rent, new and ambitious directors were ideal for such an image change; they need not be renumerated too highly and enthusiasm short-circuits questions of overtime.

The Compton Group was run by Klinger and Tony Tenser. Both were streetwise and hardnosed, from the East End Jewish milieu. Klinger was then perceived to be (and feared as) a criminal, a man with underworld connections, supposedly on good terms with the Krays, and with extensive business interests in strip clubs. He was an embodiment of that 1960s intersection of glitz and trash; in a rough cut of *Witchfinder*, during the witch-burning sequence in Lavenham, the executioner turns to his assistant and shouts 'Klinger—fetch the rope!' Such an in-joke could only be made once Tenser and Klinger had parted ways. Klinger first came across Tenser in 1960, when Tenser phoned him to hire strippers for a publicity stunt. It was a meeting of minds; Compton-Cameo Films was soon formed and an underground British flesh empire was founded: 'The godfathers of British sexploitation, Klinger and Tenser were connected in some way with virtually every sex maker in the business . . . Klinger managed London's famous Nell Gwynn strip club, and Tenser was the head of publicity for Miracle Films (he was the first to label Brigitte Bardot the "sex kitten".) In 1960 the pair went into business together to open the Compton Cinema Club.'

It was a small step from protecting smut to producing smut and in 1961 Tenser and Klinger presented *Naked as Nature Intended*, directed by Harrison Marks. It was a time when the Soho flesh trade was still fairly discreet (a necessity during those years of solid Conservative rule), but would soon come to reap the benefits of lurid revelations that fired much of the coverage of the Profumo affair. The Establishment's mistresses more often than not graduated from the Soho school, sometimes leaving damaging 8mm films, or persistent rumours of such films, behind them.

Those who worked with Klinger and Tenser were unable to tell if, ultimately, they were more interested in making films or making money. Soon the company had three London cinemas and produced and distributed Mark's subsequent 'naturist' skin flicks, and the less innocent Arnold Louis Miler and Stanley Long productions. Long and Miller were partners from the heart of the early 1960s Soho film business—strip shows, photographs (such as the views bought from under-counter photograph albums in seedy newsagents—a ritual that Michael Powell inserted into the then contemporary *Peeping Tom*), then to 8mm 'glamour films' and on to breathless exposés, shot on borrowed equipment, such as *London in the Raw* and *Primitive London* ('The jungle behind the bright lights . . . '). They formed Stag Films and claimed to dispatched one thousand prints a day at the height of business. They split in 1965 but would come to work with Mike, and Tenser, Klinger and Long were all behind Polanski's *Loveli*

Head—now called *Repulsion*. *Repulsion* and Polanski's next film *Cul-de-Sac*, embody something of this time and place; they straddle the art-exploitation divide, capitalising on the new permissiveness with explosive vulgarity. Perhaps Compton was, indeed, the only company that could back and market them at this point. Thus Polanski and Compton had given the film-going public the first (aural) female orgasm in a feature film. Tenser: 'I signed him up, signed Polanski up—because I'd read reports on *Knife in the Water*—another new director. I'd met the man. I thought he had possibilities. The script that we had was quite horrifying in its own way, but mentally so. The visuals were not horrifying but mentally so—makes you think a lot. It would scare you. He got away with quite a bit that wouldn't normally be shown because of the intensity of the film.'

Repulsion chartered a psychological odyssey through the flipside of pre-summer of love London with a supremely cool and modern sheen: isolation, madness, twisted compositions, rotting meat and a nightmare of rape, extreme close-ups, the wall that sprouts writhing arms, jazz and the fetishisation of the young Catherine Deneuve. It was soon doing the rounds of the European film festivals and picked up the Silver Bear in Berlin. Klinger hung onto the statuette; it signified Compton's successful transformation from Soho sleaze merchants to a fashionable international film outfit. For those in the know, 'Michael Klinger and Tony Tenser present . . .' and such lofty critical acclaim was incongruous to the point of hilarity. After all, it was only the impulse to have a 'respectable' wing of operations on the cheap (Repulsion cost a mere £95,000, all in) in case of problems with the police over their less salubrious films that brought Polanski into Compton's orbit in the first place.

Delighted with the *Repulsion* statuette, Klinger financed Polanski's experimental, Pinter-influenced script *If Katelbach Comes* which, as *Cul-de-Sac*, took the Golden Bear in Berlin in 1966. Both *Repulsion* and *Cul-de-Sac* received international releases and hit the American markets hard (albeit with mixed success)—and Polanski followed in their wake after the Hammer spoof *The Fearless Vampire Killers*, a score settled with the company who had initially turned him down. Klinger, now with a taste for international film production, split with the more provincial Tenser, amicably and informally, after *Cul-de-Sac*, in 1967. Tenser was finishing off *Mini Weekend* and it was at this point that he picked up Reeves, as the replacement Polanski, for *The Sorcerers*. This was to be for

Tenser's post-Klinger company, Tigon British Film Productions Ltd. Like Compton, Tigon, from its Wardour Street office, would produce and distribute. To this end, Tenser had bought a small stake in a number of West End cinema clubs, including the right to empty the slot machines of their day's takings. One of the first films that Tenser released in the UK was the unsettling American B-feature *Carnival of Souls*. Thereafter, he also released American International Pictures exploitation films, establishing a business relationship with the Californian company that would form the basis of the next Reeves film *Witchfinder General.* Tigon, able to move quicker than the bigger distributors, could provide an eclectic variety of films: who else would present Godard's *Une Femme Mariée* with *Take Your Clothes Off and Live* (directed by Miller) as a support feature.

Even when mostly out of the 'nudie' business, Tenser retained the streamlined producing skills honed during this period. He was known by his 'don't fucking worry about it' approach to pre-production, for better or worse. Yet despite this, Tenser in person was warm, concerned and jovial; he had been the approachable half of Compton. For Mike, *Revenge of the Blood Beast* showing in Kilburn was a far cry from the international distribution and acclaim that Polanski gained with Compton, so working with Tenser was a palpable opportunity.

Mike also appreciated the fast and shady Soho company. He took to hanging around the Soho offices and studios associated with Tenser, making cutting suggestions as he watched hacks slap 16mm porn together. Mike liked to be about the business of film and would have soaked up the milleu and the bustle even if he had no actual need to be in the vicinity. His auteur status can be partly attributed to this — simply, a great interest in all aspects of the film-making process.

By mid-1967 Mike was 23 and beginning to establish his haunts and habits. He had an amicable girlfriend in Annabelle, 'an archetypical sixties girlfriend. Slim. The shortest skirts from Biba. Serious too', also on the fringes of the film industry. His school contemporaries were on the bottom runs of their professions, their time organised for them, and Mike wanted a demonstrable working life too, within reason, to confirm what he did. He was able to allude to his movements in the seemingly slightly dangerous Soho underworld; when King's Mead or Radley Old Boys asked him what he was up to, he would shoot back with 'Editing the balls out of blue movies'. He would invite his friends to Yeoman's Row to watch 16mm films and chat about forthcoming film projects; 'food and drink flowed in his house—he loved having people around'. These prolonged socials became known as Mike's '"chewing-the-fat" sessions' and soon substantial crowds would be a constant. They continued in Esmerelda's Bar in Belgravia and for pub crawls down the Fulham Road. Mike enjoyed being the centre of attention; he is remembered as funny, kind and a touch mercurial, hyper and highly strung. He worked at being enigmatic, and made himself difficult to get to know—part bolshyness, and part a genuine restlessness. Phillip Waddilove, who first met Mike in 1967, recalls 'He was very much the ex-public school boy—very well mannered and extremely articulate— he certainly wasn't part of the London swinging scene of the sixties.'

Mike would switch crowds often, leave parties on a whim to lose himself in the anonymity of the streets. He would catch a late night film, stroll and take in the night air, stop for a hamburger, walk some more, return home and read film magazines. This habit would be directly transposed into *The Sorcerers*, as was his interest in cars and speed. The protagonist, the Mike alter-ego Ian Ogilvy (with the barely concealed name 'Mike Roscoe'— which Mike had altered from the original 'Mike Moore'—would pound the paving stones at night too, abandoning a group of friends for no given reason, oscillating between the company of others and his own. Mike had found himself centrally placed to explore the rapidly changing London scene during his night-time strolls. Yeoman's Row in 1967 was within the epicentre of the birth of the chemical-fuelled psychedelic underground, 'the "Swinging London" Babylon of hucksters, fixers and double-agents'— all of which held a fascination for Mike. After long nights, he would head back to Yeoman's Row, have a shot of whisky and go to bed with a F. Scott Fitzgerald short story as dawn was breaking, or would sit up fielding expected calls from America about his possible film projects.

Mike would discuss film with the earnest young Films and Filming critic David Austen—particularly in relation to the Cahiers du Cinema auteur approach to jobbing American film-makers; long, long conversations about the artistry of Howard Hawks and John Ford are recalled. Shelves and tables held piles and piles of books. Perhaps 'jobbing' was the notion that warmed Mike to the idea of *Terror for Kicks* after it had initially been shelved. Patrick took heart at the idea of the freedoms of a film made on the cheap; he decided that *Terror for Kicks* would be 'underground film-making with a bit of style', completely unfettered by studio restrictions, and the two of them put together a modest package for Tenser. Patrick and Tenser had previously done business and, post-Polanski,

Tenser was available, interested and waiting. John's 1966 *Terror for Kicks* screenplay, written in November and December, was talked up as having strong exploitation potential and squarely aimed at the lower end of the market. The deal around it would consist of a name actor, and whatever cash Patrick and Mike could muster. This would make for as good a chance as they would get.

John, Patrick, Mike and even Annabelle had brainstormed their way through the script for a number of sessions, shaping it into the modest and doable film proposition they needed. The script was the blueprint, from Tenser's point of view, for an effective remake of *The Projected Man* — but also provided a sublime idea: the notion of film as voyeurism was worked back into the story, reimagining the violence and sex (the 'kicks') as a critique of the nature of this kind of film itself. In the context of 1966 Soho, this is a very potent premise; foremost in Mike's mind would have been the desire to avoid making a film anything like those that Tigon then produced. What must have clicked when Mike read John's script was that it included within its narrative a thematic device that offered the possibility of distance for Mike and his film from the sensibility of the Soho film world; the film could be both of it, and defiantly against it. This sentiment would find its way into the film's opening; Karloff's character's advertisement is placed on a newsagent's board along with those of prostitutes. In this way, the characteristics of *Terror for Kicks* as *The Sorcerers*, are founded as much on its company of origin as was *Repulsion* — and in both these instances, this mix makes for unique film-making and films. Mike would also capitalise on the distance in terms of the wider scene; the critique would extend to swinging London — and a fair amount of John's film script was equally dismissive of the phenomenon (Mike Moore, surveying the basement club says 'Five years from now . . . There'll be a new shop, a new name — a new rave. A new generation, even. And this little lot will probably all be married and settled down by then'). Wary of the rapidly changing times, John had placed invites through the script for improvised contemporaneity in terms of music and fashions ('We see in through the window of a with-it dress shop, whatever is the rave at the time the picture is made' for example) in placing the action at the heart of London. One final connection is apparent: John's Mike was now drawn from the same mould as Mike Reeves himself; a Chelsea-based, restless young man of means, half-in, half-out of the environs in which he finds himself, studiously detached from the vagaries of fashion:

[Shot] 10 INT. BASEMENT CLUB—TWO SHOT MIKE AND PENNY NIGHT
MIKE is bored. Not ostentatiously yawning but remotely, cosmically bored. We should realise as we go on that he had practised a pose of non-involvement for so long that he had lost the ability to relax.

Even the protagonist's hip profession had been lent by the antiques dealer and Radley friend Alex Waye—drawing on the Christopher Gibbs school of London cool (and Roscoe, like Withnail, exudes the feeling that the party is somehow happening without him). Mike's friend Iain Sinclair, upon seeing the film, would see in the protagonist 'a sympathetic caricature' of Mike, via Ogilvy, now 'more than ever the director's alter ego'. The final screenplay has Roscoe describe himself at one point as 'Mercurial Mike, man of many moods'.

The Leith Productions 'chewing the fat' sessions retained their informality, even now they had been converted into full-throttle film development. Mike was preparing to make a proper film—no longer a 'Mike Reeves' film, but a 'Michael Reeves film'. John: 'We got along very well indeed in all the preliminary stages, though other work kept me from attending any shooting. I found him sociable yet sometimes distrait, if one can put it that way. He was quite impulsive, and would suddenly ring up and suggest a meeting, largely from a desire to chat rather than for any specific reason.'

Since going for broke seemed to be working, Mike saw no reason to temper his vision of the kind of film he intended to make, so it only seemed logical that Karloff should be the 'name' in the film. Mike caught up with him accordingly in Madrid, where he was guest-starring in *I Spy*. Karloff was coherent, but very old and ailing rapidly. He had contracted pneumonia in Rome while working on Bava's estimable *Black Sabbath* in 1963, was suffering from acute emphysema and beginning to glide downhill. For *The Sorcerers* he sported a metal leg brace on one arthritic leg, which had to be oiled so that the squeaking would not find its way onto the soundtrack, but was more comfortable in a wheelchair, as he also suffered from an arthritic back. Mike would have to shoot around the brace and so kept Karloff as immobile as possible (the brace is still slightly visible in some scenes). Curtis could not secure insurance for Karloff on the film. The wheelchair itself was included in a few scenes in his next film, the diabolical *Curse of the Crimson Alta* ('a strange concoction of cod H. P. Lovecraft and M. R. James, dressed up in psychedelic clothes') — uncomfortable scenes of Karloff being wheeled around the grounds of Grimsdyke House in the cold night air. For the few performances after that, Karloff came with oxygen tank too and, by most accounts, could barely talk. Karloff died on 2 February 1969.

Mike pitched the film, offered the £11,000 Karloff wanted (which, for the bedraggled gravitas alone, was a bargain) and readily agreed to accommodate Karloff's wish for script alterations. Karloff needed his character, Marcus Mesmer, a retired variety act 'mind reader', to come good in the end. This could be achieved through an eleventh-hour gesture of self-sacrifice on Mesmer's part, without Mike having to dilute the relentlessly downward spiral of the film. Tom recalls: 'In the original . . . the old folks use the transmission of sensation from the Ian Ogilvy character purely for their own gratification. No holds barred. But Karloff wouldn't buy that. He said his character had to have redeeming characteristics or he would not do it. So we turned the ending round — he putting the brakes on his wife and ultimately sacrificing himself. To save the world.'

In some ways it is surprising that Boris cared at this point, after recent appearances in films like *Bikini Beach, Die, Monster, Die!* and *Ghost in the Invisible Bikini*, but maybe he sensed that his time was near and had an urge for a swansong. In the event, he dished one out to Mike and then one to another young upstart — playing himself for Peter Bogdanovich's debut *Targets*. Why did he accept? Fee aside, the production conditions were hardly agreeable. Maybe Mike reminded him of another Englishman abroad, also film-mad and slightly depressive — the long-gone James Whale. In the days of *Bride of Frankenstein*, Karloff had to wear leg braces to deliberately degrade his ability to walk; things were coming in full circle. Mike would have known Karloff's films well, would have talked incessantly about them . . . had some experience on the pitch as a bowler, and public-school boys, of whatever epoch, speak the same language. The Uppingamian would have delivered his party piece to the Radleian by way of accepting: 'My leg in a steel brace — operating with only half a lung, why it's a public scandal that I'm still around! But as long as people want me, I feel an obligation to keep on performing. After all, every time I act I perform employment for a fleet of doubles! . . . I am never really alive unless I am at work merely recharging for the next spell. To know that I was never to work again would be something akin to a death sentence for me.' The latter sentiments were true for Mike too; another circle of sorts. For Boris, it was a chance to render a human portrait; the man whose name had become so synonymous with monster performances that Graham Greene had referred to 'the Karloff' as a type of character and acting, could now bow out on a note of humanity and redemption. Once producers had made their way to Madrid to thrash out the contract fine-print, Karloff was fully onboard. On-set he was impeccably professional. Even Tenser felt a frisson of respect for the old school: 'I can't say enough good things about Boris Karloff. He was a wonderful man, and a brilliant actor. He was nearly 80 then, but he remembered his lines and spoke them clearly. He interpreted his part absolutely correctly and uniquely, as only he could. He was the most unassuming man you could ever wish to meet. He couldn't even understand why people would want his autograph.'

The package seemed good—Curtis and Tenser struck a deal and a state of rapid pre-production was declared. There was precious little time to implement the changes Karloff needed—they would have to be made on the hoof. Curtis had been able to offer Tenser Mike, the script, half the budget already in place, agreements from Karloff and Catherine Lacey for the leading mature roles (Lacey suggested by Shaughnessy, who had just worked for her for a BBC production) and Ogilvy, of course, to play the young protagonist (who by now had something of a name on the back of a TV series, *The Liars*), and Ogilvy's RADA colleague, the actor Victor Henry. Pouty Elizabeth Ercy, who Mike was partially keen on, would fulfil the lost 'French bird' role, in the manner of Deneuve in *Repulsion* or Jaqueline Sassard in *Accident*. From Tenser, Curtis needed the other half of the budget, and help with UK and 'worldwide' marketing. It would be cheap enough all in, a total budget of £25–26,000 (including Karloff's fee)—Tenser could pick up his half of the bill with ease, mostly on pre-sales of the film, and cast a gaggle of his aspiring actresses in bit parts. Tenser's only request was that Mike pep it up a bit, make it a bit more, as *Time* magazine had it, 'London—the Swinging City'—give it some flashy footage that could be used in the trailer. The shoot would begin almost straight away, mid-January 1967, as a 'Tigon-Curtwel Global Production released through Tigon Pictures'. Karloff had clinched the deal for Tenser: 'Boris Karloff was one of the idols of my youth. I had followed his career ever since I saw *Frankenstein*, and had always been in awe of him. I had heard of Michael, and I knew he had directed an earlier low budget horror film which was successful. From the way he spoke, he seemed to have great talent. After I met with Pat a couple of more times, I knew I could trust him.' Just as Mike had schmoozed Karloff, so Tenser did too, with one eye on further films. There was flattering talk of establishing a Karloff Theatre.

The next obstacle was a meeting with John Trevelyan of the British Board of Film Censors (BBFC). Mike was mindful of the kind of reaction names like Miller and Long would provoke, and so met with Trevelyan, a distant cousin of his, under the aegis of 'Vardella Film Productions Limited' to discuss the script. Ike played the Karloff card to illustrate his seriousness. Trevelyan understood that the film would be squarely aimed at the 'X' category, and the two discussed the horror film *per se*.

Script approval was an arduous process whereby a draft script of the proposed film would be submitted to the BBFC for its blessing and advice. Trevelyan was first and foremost a diplomat, described by Peter Evans as having 'a face like a 1933 walnut case radio set: comfortable, reliable, emitting the Home Service sounds of English commonsense and autumnal bronchitis'. He relished his position with the BBFC, socialising with the likes of Ken Russell, Polanski, Andy Warhol and Paul Morrissey, pipe clamped between his teeth and a glass of red clamped in his hand. He had been with the BBFC since 1951 and by the late 1960s was easing his way into retirement, his policy of liberalisation, in 1967 at least, seemingly a quiet success. He kept a supply of whisky and Benson and Hedges in his office and would often wile away afternoons discussing the ins and outs of all the things he had seen fit to cut. He once even institutionalised this; a censorship symposium at the Royal Festival Hall, in which he showed the material he had cut from films and chatted about it at length. But he was forward looking in his appreciation of films, and held the art in high regard; by the late 1960s, his ideal films were those that combined an intellectual approach and challenging material—particularly those of Joseph Losey, Stanley Kubrick and John Schlesinger—and also understood censorship in utilitarian terms (he cut the Compton Cinema Club slack as he knew the money from their sex films was used to enable an outstanding film-maker, Roman Polanski, to make his first two feature films. Trevelyan saw himself more as an enabler than censor. He even acted as unofficial agent for Tenser at times, sending aspiring film-makers in his direction. His engagement with *Witchfinder* was far from satisfactory but, in some ways, he acted to protect the film, and shielded Tenser from the wrath expressed behind closed doors at the BBFC.

In a letter to Mike, from 3 January 1967, Trevelyan wrote: 'our general policy with regard to horror films is that there are two areas which from time to time cause us concern. These are (a) horror laced with sex, and (b) horror which goes over the edge into disgust.' In terms of his latter point, he advised Mike to shoot tamer alternative takes, particularly those for the close of the film, and to be careful with Estelle's (Lacey) 'sadism'. For Roscoe's murder of Laura, Trevelyan noted: 'Great care should be taken with these scenes. As I explained, we are advised that strangling scenes can be stimulating to certain mentally unbalanced people, so I always advise to keeping such scenes short, and if possible, without close shots. Perhaps you might even consider omitting, wholly or partly, the strangling, and leave it at a stabbing.' Tenser also had the idea about horror, and the kind of horror Tigon wanted.

How have we [come] to understand [the term] 'horror film'? The experts were Hammer Films, as they make quite a lot of them. And they really were great films: a style of horror . . . We thought we could make similar films. We did make a few films, not with Michael Reeves, but with steady directors who had made these sort of films before. You know, we watched it carefully. We made sure that all of our money was spent on the screen, and not the chauffeuring people about and what have you. Unnecessary expenses—which could be very high. These were the days when money was limited, and British films were not very attractive worldwide.

Once Tenser had his team in place, he was happy to leave Patrick Curtis to watch over the West London Studios set (he would remain 'about' on set from time to time). The crew meshed well, with everyone happy to lug the heavy equipment around between set-ups. Arnold Miller occasionally showed in his capacity as executive producer and the film would be shot by his former Stag Films partner, Stanley Long.

Long might have spent many hours shooting Soho interiors, but he was no amateur—when *Repulsion* ran over schedule, Tenser brought Long in to shoot the final third (including many of the main set-pieces). Long was able to replicate Gilbert Taylor's style—the man Kubrick used to shoot *Dr Strangelove* and whom Polanski had insisted on as the one non-negotiable 'luxury' for the *Repulsion* shoot, despite Gilbert being 'one of the most expensive cameramen in the business'. But for Polanski the film had to look expensive if nothing else; another facet of the world of *Repulsion* in which surface appearances are always deceptive. Long also simultaneously ran a film equipment rental company, an aviation company, and held a commercial pilot's license. Yet even Long, who had seen more than most in the world of exploitation film, was startled by Reeves's set decoration — he would 'go berserk on the set sometimes', drenching it in 'Kensington Gore'.

He was flinging blood about on the set like it was going out of fashion, I mean gallons of it. I used to be constantly checking him. He had this obsessive thing about throwing it up the walls, and when Susan George [as Audrey] was stabbed with a pair of scissors, it was going all over the camera, and I said 'Really, you know, come off it.' But he loved it. He seemed to revel in it. He definitely had a kink about blood.

For this sequence, Mike had devised a 'special effect': 'The knife comes into the shot again, bloody, the scene whirls as she falls. Blood spatters over the lens. A gurgle O.S . . . '. But, as Trevelyan feared, such a wildly over-the-top sequence was unacceptable and the majority of Audrey's murder did not make it to the final cut. It also left Tenser's Biba-clad young actress more than a little traumatised. Mike's unorthodox set-dressing technique, like an Impressionist squeezing paint straight out from the tube and onto the canvas, was something he would use during the *Witchfinder* shoot too: 'Mike used to walk about with a viewfinder and a blood squirter; he'd just come up and squirt it all over you. He had it with him all the time . . . He'd also come at you with scissors and cut your clothes so that there were proper bullet holes in them.'

Tenser's need for some marketable contemporaneity, Karloff's requested script changes, and Mike's tendency to map his own personality on to the incidentals of his films meant that the screenplay, although technically finished, remained something of a work in progress. Mike was immersed in pre-production, scouting for locations, and was not particularly interested in the Karloff idea of 'redemption' anyhow, and so asked John to implement Karloff's wishes in late November—could bouts of bad consciousness be put in, could the telepathy be reconfigured as a potential 'benefit to mankind' rather than just a device of heightened voyeurism, could Mesmer save the day?

Mike rang me to tell me about this, and asked for a short rewrite to accommodate Karloff's wishes, which he was entitled to do before I was paid the final small portion of my fee. I didn't much care for this distortion of the original, and as I was very busy at the time collaborating with Bill Fairchild on a TV series, I suggested he should adjust the scenes himself and I would waive my final instalment. He rang a little later to say that he had done this, but I would still get top credit.

Mike had brought Tom Baker in to make the alterations. This involved stripping down John's script, reordering some of the scenes, ejecting a third sorcerer and much of the character development (and a sequence seen from Roscoe's point of view, while under control, in which the tatty reality of a Soho knocking shop becomes wildly erotic), and a substantial car chase, which ends the film, was inserted, along with the actual streets for most of the location shots. The title was now *The Sorcerers*. For Karloff, the relatively straightforward evil-minded grotesque went and in its place came the battle of wills between (as he was now called) Professor Marcus Monserrat and his wife Estelle, and his former profession upped to a 'medical hypnotist'. He was no more akin to a fallen cousin of Professor Bernard Quatermass. After this process, Tom got a generously large credit for his work, and John was disappointed to find that he had been unfairly been reduced to a status of 'mere supplier of an idea', despite the promise of top credit.

Whereas in John's script the Monserrats had just utilised telepathy and a series of potions to gain control of Roscoe, the redrafting wedged in a scene of psychedelic brainwashing to meet Tenser's request for flashy footage. John's script had originally left space for new trends, but patterned the telepathy on Mike's addiction to the daily potions that the sorcerers gave him. This addiction would have suggested drug use to Mike and Tom and, by the time the film was in production, the logical step was to link this reading with the emergent dope and LSD-fuelled scene; in the small space between John's original script (outline 1965; script mid-1966) and the production (early 1967), everything had changed. It is no surprise that, riffing off the changing times, the brainwashing sequence came to parallel the experiences of the emerging underground London scene, and recontextualises the film accordingly. Mike's nocturnal explorations were paying off—a liquid light show, coupled with what John later referred to as the 'tinpot B-move gadgetry' was introduced; Mike had stumbled across the Pink Floyd and the Spontaneous Underground, that occurred in the Marquee Club in Soho on dates throughout 1966. The Soho underground was both pornographic and psychedelic.

The Pink Floyd had emerged at the point when acid eclipsed hashish as the drug of choice, at the turn of 1966, and provided the soundtrack to a new consciousness, then concentrated specifically in Mike's London stomping grounds. By the end of 1966, with a gig in the Roundhouse and a stay at the Tottenham Court Road UFO Club (both 'Unidentified Flying Object' and Underground Freak-Out') and the Pink Floyd were an obligatory event, finding themselves forging their own mythology, culminating in the 14 Hour Technicolour Dream in Alexandra Palace in April 1967. LSD fired the cutting-edge music/media events which had to be experienced. *Astronomie Domine* and the 'Blob Show', the 'Giant Mystery Happening', or the Sensual Laboratory at the UFO Club in collaboration with The Soft Machine.

Mike's fascination with the evolving scene would have been amply rewarded. In the jam-packed basement, a sweltering art school and hippie crowd, kitted out in the boutique fashions of Granny Takes A Trip, would get stoned or drop acid and give themselves up to the spooky sounds of the psychedelic space jams, turning their minds over to the hypnotic strobes and liquid wheel light shows. The music did not interest Mike as much as the sonics and the event itself—something which Michael Horovitz referred to as 'the new solar sound-systems of beat caverns, pop charts and psychedelic "trips"'. Despite the psychedelic pretentions to visualise an under-the-influence 'experience', the events were, as Kubrick, Siegel, Michelangelo Antonioni, Peter Whitehead and others also noted, eminently cinematic. Allowing psychedelia to infiltrate *The Sorcerers*, particularly after opening club scenes that grate with their unhipness, would lend an authenticity to the world of the film, would dally with the subversive in a way that few horror films could have accommodated before.

Psychedelia depended primarily on visual disturbances, anamorphoses and what could be called the perspectives of the narcosis. The debt to a certain satanic English Romanticism of the early nineteenth century, evident in contemporary dandyism ad a revival of the occult, could entail a condition which de Quinc[e]y had recognized, in visual experience: 'Space swelled and was amplified' [in *Confessions of an English Opium Eater*].

Casting the psychedelic experience as the telepathy-brainwashing element in the film aligned the film to the subjective sensibility of the psychedelic happening, only months after the scene first emerged (it was so close that Mike had to explain was 'psychedelia' was). *The Sorcerers* does not grind to a halt before the surface of the London scene, diligently recording the fashions, the sounds and the locations of choice, as so many films were to, but works the sensibility into the film so as to attempt to penetrate the scene and gauge what lies behind. Mike squirts psychedelia over the film at close range, much as he had done with the Kensington gore. In this respect and in terms of Roscoe's hidden psychopathic identity, the population of *The Sorcerers* is not unlike that of the invite for a Pink Floyd gig at the Spontaneous Underground in February 1966: 'Who will be there? Poets, pop singers, hoods, Americans, homosexuals (because they make up 10 per cent of the population), 20 clowns, jazz musicians, one murderer, sculptors, politicians and some girls who defy description, are among those invited.'

In the pseudo-religious ceremony that the Floyd's Syd Barrett presided over, all the activity merged into one oceanic pulse—black mass and psychedelic be-in, the new sound and the new consciousness: the happening. This is what Mike needed to recreate. He located Joe Gannon, then taking his light show from club to club. Gannon had worked with the Floyd in the early days of the Spontaneous Underground and had been the driving force behind the use of film, projected onto the wall behind the band, to supplement the colour slides. Much of his equipment was plucked from the rubbish tips of closing West End theatre shows, rewired and set up on his rig. Mike arranged for Joe to bring his equipment into a studio in Barnes to shoot the sequence. This was to be horror with no worrying about stage blood, costumes, skewering . . . this time it could be music, lights, zooming, wires, dials, and Karloff as Syd Barrett, or like some demented DJ, would preside over the psychedelic chaos; 1960s meets 1930s, the swinging mad scientist, the swelling and amplification of space. There is a kind of logic to it; for the Beatles and their 'Turn off your mind, relax and float downstream' Karloff offers 'Relax, clear your mind, empty your mind of all thoughts' as he starts up the psychedelic brain-washing machine, its sound mimicking the Pink Floyd wall of sound prolonged UFO jams.

Mike expressed a keen awareness of this contemporaneity, even acknowledging the limitations of immersion in such a close reality, via Austen, in *Films and Filming*, where *The Sorcerers* was described as 'The film's surface appearance will date quickly, for it is so securely anchored at this particular crossroads of space and time. But anyone in the future seeking an accurate reference to the quintessence and mores of the "now" generation will find it here far more so that in some other recent films ostensibly concerned with this.' Mike even puts a reminder *in* the film of the distance between it and that which had previously passed as youth films; in Nicole's flat, Cliff Richard's *In the Country* warbles from a Dansette record player. But memories of *The Young Ones* and *Summer Holiday* are soon banished once Roscoe beds her. She pulls Roscoe down on top of her, into the foreground, as the camera pans down; a dissolve later and she's found in a pose of studied post-coital nonchalance, much like Steele. It would seem that Mike was even honing his film director's eye in the bedroom.

In *The Sorcerers*, psychedelia is contextualised in terms of the darker currents in underground culture and its antecedents. Professor Monseratt's quasi-scientific interest in hypnosis, the séance-like table across which the Monserrats exert psychic control of Roscoe, and his wife's witch-like qual-ities, denote the way in which 'witchcraft . . . [had] become an eccentric adjunct to sixties pop culture'. Mike is a believer in the psychedelic ethos, and so warns against it from that vantage point — he is a summer of love heretic rather than atheist. This rejection of the fledgling philosophy of swinging London places *The Sorcerers* a considerable distance from those films gearing up to exploit the myth or revelling in it, as Austen would note in the review. For Mike, the set of *Performance*, for example, with its art school bohemians, high pretentions (an unchecked exploration of 'the transforming quality of hallucinogens on the collective consciousness . . . ') and Cecil Beaton snapping away, would have been of little interest. The psychedelic sequences in *The Sorcerers* still indicate the ways in which liquid light shows were 'attempted analogues for narcotic experiences . . .' but here, rather than opening up the mind, they work to shut it down — control rather than freedom, blackouts rather than hallucinations: a trap, not a trip. The brainwashing also pushed the film into science fiction territory, with the same 'it could be happening now' vision of the future that Siegel offered in *Invasion of the Body Snatchers*. As British science fiction, *The Sorcerers* is also vastly as odds with the general trends, as outlined by Hunter.

Conciously or otherwise, the film rebuts the notion, then in the air, of the dawning of a new, cosmic consciousness and the recommended 'giving in to strange forces'—seeing in the age of Aquarius not the summer of love, but the civil unrest of 1968, Altamont, the Manson murders and the shattering of the mantras of peace, love and harmony. Mike would engage again with this theme in *Witchfinder*, fashioning an equally circumnavigational reaction to the times.

In person, Mike only expressed distaste for the hippies, their drugs and happenings—they represented a degree of liberation that Mike perceived to be self-centeredness disguised as revolutionism. Tom recalls 'Mike and I had a long recurring argument about selfishness. He maintained that all human action was at base selfish. I held that altruism was possible. I think I came of my own opinion as much from hope as experience. But I could never shift him from his position. It wasn't something that depressed him. It was just something that he could see, he would say, even if others were not prepared to face it.' Mike would have felt a measure of distance from the UFO crowd, though this and through his reticence about acid use and entering into the spirit of such an event; 'open yourself up' for someone slightly intense and depressive would have sounded more like bad advice—Mike's karma was in short supply at the best of times. He had sufficient cynicism to see through the revolutionary posturing, but the experience could not have made anything other than a substantial impact, and demanded some kind of response. This was, after all, his generation, even if Mike preferred American music (of course), did not wear the gear, and was a confirmed puritan about any drug use. For Mike, all the talk of changing the world was slightly ridiculous, paisley power just another fad, 'legalise pot' neither here nor there. More to the point, as the hippies got stoned, the war in South East Asia intensified, unimpeded by the 'professed apolitical stance of the average flower child'. Mike would attempt to grasp this contradiction in psychological rather than ideological terms, attempt to understand and pin down a collective mindset. It was easy to see who constituted the psychedelic underground, and why, from the vantage point of Yeoman's Row, but to understand the dovetailing of two seemingly mutually contradictory narratives in early 1967 (peace, love and harmony, and better dead than red) was a pressing, more engaged task. This interest in the place of violence in society had informed Mike's attraction to the film in the first place, was evident in *Intrusion*, and would now be readdressed. To draw such a film from the London scene was to find the murder in the psychedelia, and the psychedelia in the murder. Such connections were tentatively being made in other areas, with Internationalism as the bridge that connected the war zone to the peace zone, and this sensibility would flourish in 1968. But Internationalism, even in the unification of dissent against imperialist slaughter, functioned to locate the problems outside the collective consciousness—they remained something 'over there'. Mike would attempt to draw the problem into the heart of the London scene.

Monserrat's experiments are presented as both operating and experiencing a psychedelic light show, and Roscoe is complicit in his own reconfiguring. The sequence reproduces the ambiguity that Mike experienced in the UFO Club; Roscoe's underground freak-out controlled by Monserrat's white-interior Unidentified Flying Object-like lab, referred to as 'The Psychedelic Room' in the final shooting script:

59. ON MIKE VERY CLOSE
As the beam hits him. The lights moving over his face now are a shifting hallucination. The sound, reverberating through the headphones into his eardrums, is a shattering mixture of discords that modulate terrifying into one another without ceasing—and all the time getting stronger and more piercing.

Here, LSD and film are both reduced to their common denominator: false experience for those hungry for experience. And Roscoe, who cuts a dapper figure in the new London in a variety of turtlenecks, his time his own, women there for the taking, the nightclub offering a vista of possible pleasures, becomes a victim of the psychedelic body snatchers. Despite the proofs of freedom all around him, his mind is no longer his own.

John was horrified when he saw these unwieldy sci-fi happenings wedged into his polished script in favour of other, more important parts, now missing—mostly the development of the dramatic trajectory whereby the Monserrats become addicted to the compulsion to experience more and more and the 'gradually cumulative menace, which Mike vulgarises over and over again'. It was apparent in the 'brilliance of the direction and editing' that the film could have been restrained and made for a complete realisation of the script and its central concept, but it would seem that Mike had seen, in John's script, something that was not there to begin with, and had run with that impulse during production. *Terror for Kicks* had been 'used . . . as a vehicle for a sequence of gimmicks—some quite brilliant, apart from his Schoolboy's Own Electricity Kit'. The revised script, done by Mike and Tom, was indulgent and lacked John's polish and precision, but represented a challenge, the kind of thing Mike could rise to and use to explore spur-of-the-moment ideas, rather than John's script, which represented a good film that would simply need to be well made.

The rapidity with which the film moved into production caused immediate problems. The crew lacked sufficient experience to work under the limitations of such a low budget (so small as to be unrealistic from the outset) in a high-pressure environment. Yet Mike would make no concessions in terms of how scenes were to be shot, and he planned an impossible shooting schedule to give the film the kind of scope he wanted; 'endless locations were drawn up' all over London, lengthy night shoots planned, weeks' worth of set-ups crammed into days. Even shuttling the crew from one location to another could not be done in the time that Mike had allotted for it. Perhaps of the easy-going nature of the Maslansky films, where hard slog and collective long days were all that was needed to overcome production shortcomings, Mike remained unaware of the factory-line nature of exploitation film shoots. It was a naivety that was crippling and for Long, who had ample experience, Mike was 'a very inexperienced director out of his depth'. This was apparent in his lack of understanding of the technical aspects of film-making (although working in such circumstances would have been a baptism of fire for even the most able), which soon rendered Mike highly insecure on the set and unable to see that his expectations and demands for perfection were going to be the film's undoing. All of Long's practical suggestions—handheld shots rather than dollies, conversations in one shot rather than reverse angle shots—were unequivocally rejected as compromises that Mike was unwilling to take. It became Mike's defining characteristic as the director: 'Mike Reeves was a person who would not compromise.' This extended to the cast as well; while shooting Karloff across the floor, then lifting himself up to look directly into the camera (for the sequence in which he looks impotently on as Estelle smashes up the laboratory equipment with his walking stick — 'I'll stop you if it's the last thing I do'), Mike demanded one take too many. The ancient actor crawled across the floor as required for the umpteenth time, looked into the camera and asked 'How much fucking longer?'.

Long could see that Tenser believed in Mike's abilities, but the situation had conspired to place Mike in an impossible position. And Mike, who felt he had made every compromise in order to get the film made in the first place, and had hatched the plan long before Tenser and crew were invited on board, found that the film that he had set out to make was now deemed to be a film that could not be made. One week into the projected four-week (maximum) shoot, an emergency meeting was called in the Park Lane Hilton for Tenser, Patrick Curtis, Mike and Long. Mike's schedule for the following week was impossible — a 'totally ridiculous task' — and could not be implemented; not even Long, a highly proficient lighting cameraman used to working at speed, could work *that* fast. At best, the film would fall behind schedule and go massively over-budget; at worse, the film would not be completed at all. Mike, still unable to accept possible compromise, objected to suggestions of scaling back the production; since it was necessary to get key scenes in the can, why not just shoot them outdoors as he intended to? Why use any old alleyway for the nightclub murder when he had found an ideal one elsewhere? Long, unhappy to find himself cast in the opposition to the idealists on set, pointed out the insurmountable technical problems with Mike's unrealistic schedules in relation to the budget and the size of the crew. His expectations were way out of kilter; there were only so many hours of darkness each night; forty set-ups in six locations across two nights was impossible. Mike, initially insecure and upset, was now in tears. Tenser was very fond of Mike and rather paternal toward him, and Mike found he was able to handle Tenser and respected him. For Tenser, Mike was quiet and unassuming — 'the last word in a dictionary he would understand was "ego"'. So the film would be made; a new schedule drawn up for a truncated version of the film as originally planned. This reduced the action in the final screenplay to less complicated sequences but also whittled down the wordiness of the Baker/Reeves rewrite, which contained an abundance of expositional dialogue. Long would assist in the implementation and Tenser, who had been known to truncate film productions by tearing random pages from their shooting scripts, was firm in his backing of Mike's revised vision.

However, not even this scaling back salvaged the film's production from the fundamental budgetary problems, resulting in a film costing twice as much as originally planned, mostly because of a vast shooting ration. Despite Mike's stylistic perfectionism, in terms of its aesthetic, the film looks like its budget—particularly the interiors (other than those in the Monserrat flat), which are often blasted with unsympathetic light. Many critics expressed dismay at the execution when seeking out and viewing *The Sorcerers* after first seeing *Witchfinder* (for Wood, *The Sorcerers* is at once 'the finest of his films in conception and worst in execution'). The night location shots work well though; uncluttered, neon against the inky, starless sky, and a selection of dank back alleys which provide Roscoe with an apt Jack the Ripper setting.

From the second week onwards, the shoot moved with extra speed. As with *Revenge of the Blood Beast*, Mike worked hard on those sequences that he knew could be outstanding, and gave way on the filler. The formal procedures of location work were the last thing on anyone's mind and so the most non-studio sequences were made without any permissions whatsoever. Where permissions were applied for and denied (the Dolphin Square Hotel swimming pool, for example), bribes were freely used (£20 in this case, to a night guard). The opening scene (in the South Kensington night club, Blaises) was shot as rapidly as possible because of the cost of the mini skirted extras. Once the scene was ready, and the band playing (the short lived R&B group Lee Grant and the Capitols, lip synch-fronted by Mike's friend and sometimes lodger Dani Sheridan), all hands were on deck, the crew snatching whatever glimpses of flesh they could (and you could guarantee that Long's crew would be doing so). Even Patrick found himself lying on the floor of the nightclub, filming upwards as the extras gyrated (until he caught sight of his wife's face looming into the camera viewfinder). Street shots were filmed from an old taxi that Tenser had bought for the shoot (and sold for a profit after it), while the chase sequences used Patrick's Rolls Royce Convertible, *sans* top. For the motorcycle scenes, shot without permission on the A4, Mike placed himself in the boot of the speeding car, beneath the camera, yelling directions to Ogilvy to 'come closer'. It was only a matter of time before the police caught up with the production—and fortunately this did not occur until the very end of the shoot. The scene was the final moment of the film; Roscoe perishes as his car crashes and bursts into flames. An old bomb site in Notting Hill was located and the effects man told on the sly to put as much petrol in the car's tank as possible. Mike noting that 'if 10 gallons are good, 50 will be even better'. The car was ignited and the resultant explosion was so big that it blew out all of the house windows all around. In a scene anticipated on the railway tracks during Radley film-making days as Mike and friends scarpered on their bicycles, the entire crew, now temporarily without hearing, scrambled to pack up the equipment and clear out in the knowledge the police cars, ambulances and fire engines had already been dispatched. By the time they arrived, Mike had long gone, but those who had been unable to get away found their names were taken.

Tenser allotted a little more than a week for post production, a strategy for ensuring that his aspiring auteurs do not have the time to indulge in perfectionism. Mike oversaw the cutting with Ralph Sheldon, whom Patrick had called in after he had worked in Rome on the Welch film *The Biggest Bundle of Them All*. Time was so tight that Ralph and Mike had to cut reel by reel—sending individual reels away as they were done so that the negative could be cut and work started on the dubbing, overseen by Ralph's assistant, David Woodward. They were unable to see a fine cut right through. Ralph, nervous of what the finished product might look like, was happy to leave for another commitment, handing over to Woodward, and to allow others to take the screen credit for the editing. When Tenser asked why, he replied 'You wouldn't expect Rembrandt to sign an unfinished piece.' When the first cut was ready, a Wardour Street preview cinema was hired for the screening, with Tenser and Trevelyan present. From a running time of 90-95 minutes, Tenser asked for 10 to be cut (no reason was offered), and so beginnings and ends of scenes were trimmed, no sequences were removed entirely.

Stealing shots, location shooting and cutting loose from both studio setting and the script made for elements in the film that push against the more conventional aspects of *The Sorcerers*. The film sees a dialectical struggle between the thrills and freedoms drawn from Mikes guerrilla film-making, and the excellence of the realisation of the conventional trajectory of the script, each element periodically threatening to overwhelm the other. The film's resultant freshness and ability to surprise, in spite of the datedness of so many of the settings, can be attributed to this, and the continual juxtapositioning of the two narratives through the intercutting (most dramatic in terms of the sound), keeps the film on edge. The only scenes that drag are those in the basement club; bad dancing, groping extras (sexless in that way unique to British cinema), 'clever' repartee. Unfortunately, the nightclub becomes the regular meeting place for the protagonists, just as the film regroups itself by retreating back there too on several occasions. Roscoe's friends, Alan (Henry) and Nicole (Ercy), also inhabit this milieu and are equally uninteresting—she two-dimensional, little more than a model peeled off the pages of the *Nova* magazine that Roscoe leafs through in her flat, and he kitted out in tweed jacket, seemingly and inexplicably like Dylan Thomas during his lost London years. Once Roscoe has taken off on his killing spree, the Monserrats in tow, and before the police proceduaral strain of the narrative kicks in, these two wander around commiserating with each other and continually representing little more than dead-air.

The Monserrats are a latter-day Adam and Eve, He still broods over the yellowed clippings of a tabloid exposé that saw him hounded out of business many years before, and has the air of the persecuted Wilhelm Reich in exile, or a benign Aleister Crowley in his dying years. She has endured years of humble living in their dingy flat as a result. So the Garden of Eden that the telepathy machine represents offers a new beginning—a chance to relive youth, to sample the newfound freedoms of the 1960s. Despite their age, they are now no longer locked into the logic of Larkin's dour perspective of things in *Annus Mirabilis* and can plunge headlong into the world of pills, porn, sex and violence that the film constructs. Even Alan's garage foreman (Mike's regular stuntman Alf Joint, whom he had met during *The Long Ships*) feels that he had missed the boat in terms of the new, youth-orientated world, commenting 'wish I was your age' over Alan's plans to meet up with Nicole. However, this being 1967 BBFC rather than 1967 AD, the film cannot make good on such a promise; Estelle initially uses Roscoe as a personal shopper (whereas in John's version he heads straight for a prostitute) and they both enjoy the sensations of some innocent swimming. The obvious sensual kick—sex—only occurs when Roscoe is tuned out. But the violence is there; Estelle alternating between whimpering and commanding Roscoe on, their gestures mirrored and deftly cut together. The experience revitalises her—a caterpillar-to-butterfly performance, sparkling eyes greedy for further sensation. What goads her on? Female empowerment as she spars with her psychologically weaker husband?; material gain, initially (middle-class aspirations?), then drunkenness by the close of the film (middle-class comeuppance(; a lust for those sensations denied to her generation, to be 'Someone young [like] all these children out on the streets at night, taking pills to keep themselves awake'—a return of the repressed?; original sin revisited, albeit with the genteel elderly replacing Golding's youth of *Lord of the Flies*? All these possible readings gather under the Reevesian preoccupation of the potential for man to find within the propensity for violence.

The temptation is to read the Monserrats as personifications of Roscoe's already-present psychotic tendencies, 'these moods of his' as Alan calls them, the 'bloody artistic temperament'; the Monserrats as the witches to Roscoe's Macbeth, capitalising on the existential angst that indicates a volatile ad possible violent character from the outset. Roscoe's behaviour under hypnosis is in keeping with his prior traits—ditching Nicole for no reason, antagonising Alan for little gain. Hutchings notes this, Sinclair configures his reading of the film around it, so that 'The interest is in the vivid demonstration of the Reeves thesis; how Ogilvy . . . is pushed from ennui towards unmotivated acts of violence; how there is no redemption, no way of sidestepping fate.' Pirie expands upon such a reading too: 'For the other characters, including Mike's girlfriend, the film is about psychopathy . . . And on yet another level it could be regarded as a study of schizophrenia (the old couple are Mike's parents or superego "inside his head"). This had also been present in John's screenplay; schizophrenia is mentioned as Mike's friends look at his corpse (after plunging into a fire on a building site), confessing that they cannot understand his behaviour, and Alan dismisses Mike's talk of others controlling him as 'phantoms of his imagination'.

In terms of the film itself, however, the reverse seems truer in citing one of the narratives as a metaphoric subtext accounting for the other; the film tilts in Monserrats' favour in terms of realism. They live alone in a lived-in flat, a setting worthy of any of the realist movements of British post-war film, while it is Roscoe alone who engages in fantastical experience sprees, coded in the manner of the tabloid imagining's of today's youth—pills and sex, nightclubs and hedonism, and the lack of moral shame that is the price of the recent onset of classlessness (and classlessly, Roscoe even drops common inflections into an otherwise pristine accent). After all, the film pointedly strips Karloff of his make-up, grand entrances and star status— opening with the self-effacing Karloff as Karloff in ridiculously drab surroundings; Greene would have approved. Since the Monserrats anchor the film in the realm of realism, Roscoe is left as a better candidate for that of metaphor. This 'cipher' status is the thematically looped back into the film, since despite the ambiguity of a metaphor-as-characterisation, the film is constructed around Ogilvy's young protagonist. As the question of Roscoe's role in the film (that is, determining forces that make up the actual character) remain unanswered, something constantly voiced by Nicole and Alan, this 'metaphoric' ambiguity defaults to thematic ambiguity, and the result is Roscoe's blankness and boredom, his 'blackouts', his unengagedness with the world around—he remains an undercertainly animated vessel for the desires of others. Even his vestiges of personality seem more drawn from the idea of who he thinks he should be than who he actually is. This then makes sense of his near-immediate willingness to follow Professor Monserrat back to his flat, even at the point when talk of 'complete abandonment with no thought of remorse . . . intoxication with no hangover, ecstasy with no consequence' seems entirely concerned with the liberalisations of the 1967 Sexual Offences Act—despite Roscoe's sexism and machismo, here indications of an aggressive heterosexuality. In this way, Roscoe is both a blank canvas and the centre of the world of the film by dint of his freedom, youth and attractiveness, and the way that the characters, and the camera, choose to follow him. The character comes to resonate with a sense of Mike's sense of gut-reaction critique of the generation who too willingly embrace a code of the annihilation of the self, as also manifest in the hippie philosophy, buying into the 'multicoloured miracles' and 'dazzling, indescribable experiences' without a second thought, shirking a responsibility to take control of their own destinies (an idea dramatised in the film with Roscoe's literal loss of physical and mental control). He is both everyman and, in the manner of Eliot, hollow man.

The cutting together of the Roscoe and Monserrat narratives recalls a similar parallel in *Revenge of the Blood Beast*. Mike cuts between Vardella (as she attacks Van Helsing) and the innkeeper watching television, both grotesque and laughing hideously, the juxtaposition suggesting an association between the characters of the she-beast and the innkeeper. She attacks Van Helsing and he will shortly attempt rape. It is another form of possession, the 'dark side' in ascendence—akin to the idea of Vardella as the flip-side of Veronica. Like a variation on the original ending for *Blood Beast*, now back in London, Roscoe turns into a monster, dragging the singer Laura, (Sheridan) out of the nightclub, down a dark alleyway and strangling her, and slaughtering Audrey. As Estelle gains the upper hand in the telepathic battle between the Monserrats, a new parallel for Roscoe emerges; both he and Marcus lose autonomy and are reduced, to puppets of Estelle's will. The precedents then become apparent; they both feel cut off from the world around them, share the same restlessness and so pace the streets at night, they both reside in similar environments—Roscoe's antique shop packed with the same dusty bric-a-brac as the Monserrat's flat—and, iconically, both are stars in the Mike Reeves horror firmament. It is from this vantage point that Marcus realises that he must utilise his understanding of this parallel to defeat Estelle; he notices the stigmata facet of the telepathic communication, the cuts on the Monserrats' hands, shared with Roscoe—and that therefore physical sensations can be physically manifest too in a reciprocal telepathic connection. Roscoe's 'awakening' seconds before his death, as Marcus exerts his mental control, and then Roscoe's final scream as the car crashes (expressions of his last-minute regaining his ability to act independently) denotes a small measure of cooperation in the 'ultimate sacrifice' death pact he strikes with Marcus to destroy the common enemy.

There is little question that the real monster in this film is woman, now given the power to act independently, outside the historically assigned roles; the Eve who first tempts with illicit delights and then destroys essentially decent males. Hutchings assembles a reading of the film along such lines, typical of analyses of horror films; 'one can place alongside these representations of a troubled heterosexual masculinity the presence of several independent women' and that 'it is the prospect of a woman actively desiring rather than being the desired object that it [the film] finds so alternatively so appalling and so enthralling . . .'. In this way, the destructive force in the film is the return or revenge of a primal feminity, a she-beast, where female autonomy is codified in sexual terms and gestures (Hutchings notes the reference to the contraceptive pill in relation to generically liberated French girl Nicole and a telling cut to the barren Estelle in the context of this allusion to potential reproductive capacity)—sexually wanton, or just wanton in the terms of destruction (the 'King Kong syndrome'). When Estelle fails to find any connection to the female victims of Roscoe's rampages, this 'depoliticises' the film along the lines of such a gender reading. Thus, the notion of a monstrous female is demonstrable in terms of the unconscious constructions and prejudices of the film, making the film another apt candidate for 'the standard critique of horror as straight-forward sadistic misogyny'.

The conscious 'meaning' of the film, on the other hand, is one that so blatantly suggests itself that all subsequent critics have taken up the invitation to elaborate on it: the modus operandi of the sorcery is, in fact, little more than the heightened experience of cinema itself. Pirie, for example, concludes that 'the last shot of *The Sorcerers* is logically the burning of the cinema where the film is being shown', It is a reading that originates with Mike himself (via Austen in the *Film and Filming* review):

The real weight comes from the extent to which [the telepathy] is analogous to cinematic sublimation ... They entice a young man to be their guinea-pig, explaining that he will be mesmerised 'with the aid of light and the use of sound' and that he will be able to feel 'intoxication without a hangover, and ecstasy with no consequence.' That sounds awfully like the cinema, and the questions that the film triggers off about a vicarious experiences soon trap one in a mirror maze of identification.

These questions, as noted by Wood, are ones that imply that the film audience is guilty by proxy—cheering on the destruction from the safety of their seats, which may be film-fantasy destruction, but supposedly taps into that real hidden reserve of 'perverted and sadistic desires' that is personified in Estelle. All drafts of the screenplay call for subliminal shots of Estelle beckoning Roscoe on, aligning her desires with the effect that such shots would mimic. In this respect, the film is almost a dramatisation of BBFC policy towards the dangers of horror, '... stimulating to certain mentally unbalanced people'. However, mapping the invited reading on to the unconscious one produces a provocative synthesis: that cinema itself is a feminine-like entity since it entices with the promise of illicit thrills, and—in another stereotypical female behavioural trait—then refuses to let go, dragging everything towards destruction. The addictive and terminal vicarious identifications suggests that the danger is not that of (as advertised) 'no consequence' but quite the reverse—one of true vicarious experiences'; the experience of gaining secondary pleasure by primarily pleasuring a loved female. Certainly, much of the texture of the interactions of the film work in this fashion: Roscoe keeps Estelle on the point of orgasm-like quivering and whimpering for a fair part of the film's duration. The final crash is an orgasmic release, the climax of vicarious thrill-seeking, the severing of the connection and a shared *petite mort* for all those concerned, and the film itself ('The End'). Thus the fear of women as intrinsically destructive is displaced on to an ambiguous view of cinephilia; cinema first entices with a promise of quick satisfaction, and then release itself to be a true object of love once the spell has been cast— and the consequences will follow in the void of loss of control for those who step in. In this respect, cinephilia seems as suspect as the psychedelia that the film rounds on; both are false gods since both dupe reality, opiates that render 'space swelled and . . . amplified' and false, that deny a perspective on the real world.

In ways already noted, the film invites a biographical reading too. For Mike to situate the film itself at the heart of *The Sorcerers*, just as film was the centre of his world and the thing that defined him, and then to track the destruction and chaos that follows, seems to express a fear of the completeness of his own identification with film. He seems to cite himself inadvertently as also open to the dangers that he sees in those, less exacting, who follow the hippie philosophies. Mike's doom-laden alter-ego is, and not for the last time, physically destroyed by the close of this process. Mike had placed himself in *The Sorcerers* and allowed the film to access himself. Like a dream recounted for the purpose of psychoanalysis, the film had found and expressed things that Mike himself had not yet realised or articulated; the film had controlled and lived vicariously through him, drawing on his experiences to make it real, determining his emotions and actions, as would the next film, to leave behind the juvenile realm and weaken the sorcery of film over him, to move into the next period of filmmaking where mike May still get his fingers burnt, but not be totally engulfed by flames. Mike had recognised himself as an innocent, prone to a powerful form of sorcery.

Boris was overjoyed when *The Sorcerers* opened in the West End in June 1967. It was the first Karloff film to have done so in many years. To Tenser's delight, it was selected as the British entry for the Sixth International Festival of Science Fiction in Trieste, where it picked up the Golden Asteroid in June 1968; a Silver Asteroid went to Catherine Lacey (despite her strong dislike for the film and her part), and a specially created award went to Boris. It also took the Grand Prix at the San Sebastian Science Fiction Film Festival and picked up tidy notices in the US trade press, under Patrick's astute marketing. It was sold to Allied Artists and opened in the US in January 1968. In Germany, it opened as *Im Banne des*

Dr Monserrat ('The Spell of Dr Monserrat'—shades of the venerable Drs Caligari and Mabuse), in Spain as *Los Brujos* (a direct translation), in Italy as *Il Killer di Satana* and in France as *La Creature Invisible* ('L 'Ultime Creation de Boris Karloff).

When some British reviewers failed to rave, Mike marshalled Austen to pen a polemical appreciation of *The Sorcerers* for the October 1967 edition of the middlebrow UK film magazine Film and Filming. It would also be a UK heads-up for the precocious emerging talent—then shooting *Witchfinder*. The piece sounds like it was cooked up in Mike's front room, Mike's role changing from that of feeding Austen production facts to over-seeing a part-defence of the film, part press-release for it:

It makes me heartily sick to hear of complaints about the dearth of young talent in this country and the poor quality of British produced films (the few that there are nowadays) and then to witness the recep-tion accorded this picture. To be fair, a handful of 'daily' reviewers highly commended it but the remaining majority of film journalists either ignored it or wrote it off in a brusque paragraph. The facts in the case of *The Sorcerers* are that it was made (a) by a young Englishman, 23-year-old Michael Reeves, and (b) produced by a new British company for the remarkably realistic budget (one of the few there are nowadays) of £40,000. For these facts alone the film deserves sympathetic attention and constructive criticism. These remarks are in no way intended as special pleading, for this picture needs no apologists.

Mike Reeves, the director of *The Sorcerers*, is certainly no appren-tice. His background includes time spent in Hollywood, assisting in the production of some well-know mini-epics, script-writing, and his own promising first feature . . . I understand the independently produced *Sorcerers* is getting bookings from both major circuits, which is an encouragement and, I hope, a spur to further films from smaller companies willing to give young talent a chance to prove itself.

The review goes on to praise the performances and the construction of the film (especially the cross-cutting).

Curtis used the profits to develop further pictures, including Welch as a Mata Hari in *Mademoiselle Docteur*, and *The Devil's Discord* was dusted off and put back into development. But Tony Tenser had other, and immediate plans for Mike.

Liner Notes from "The Sorcerers" DVD

Kim Newman

B ORN IN 1944, MICHAEL REEVES WENT FROM AN ENGLISH
public school (Radley), where he dabbled in filmmaking with class-
mate Ian Ogilvy, to the nether regions of the film industry. Semi-famous
for turning up unannounced at the Hollywood home of his idol, Don
Siegel, and landing a job shooting ingenue auditions for the Elvis Presley
Western *Flaming Star* (1960), Reeves had enough family money to
finance jaunts to Yugoslavia to land work as a minion on Jack Cardiff's
Viking mini-epic *The Long Ships* (1964), then to Rome to do direct
second-unit on *Il castello dei morti vivi* (*Castle of the Living Dead*, 1964),
a gothic horror film starring Christopher Lee and a young Donald Sutherland, credited to Italian Luciano Ricci (aka 'Herbert Wise') but actually
directed by American Warren Kiefer (after whom Sutherland named his
son). Hooking up with producer Paul Maslansky, later of the *Police
Academy* films, Reeves made his directorial debut with a vampire movie
starring Barbara Steele (who had been fired from *Flaming Star*) and the
inevitable Ogilvy, *La sorella di Satana* (aka *Revenge of the Blood Beast* or
The She Beast, 1965). Returning to London, Reeves made only two further
features—*The Sorcerers* (1967) and Matthew Hopkins, *Witchfinder
General* (1968)—before his death in February 1969 of an overdose of
prescription drugs.

The Sorcerers began with a complex deal between several interesting
film industry 'characters'. Reeves, eager to make something more
'personal' and yet still commercial, hit upon a science fiction/horror story,
'Terror for Kicks' by John Burke – who remains best known for 'novelising'
a string of film and TV scripts (anything from *Look Back in Anger* and *A*

Hard Day's Night and through *Dr. Terror's House of Horror* and *Privilege* to *Dad's Army* and *The Bill*), but also edited the occasional anthology (*Tales of Unease*) and contributed original stories to Herbert van Thal's long-running *Pan Book of Horror Stories* series. Reeves bought the rights and worked up a script with credited but apparently minimal input from his long-time associate Tom Baker (not the actor), put up some of his own money and secured matching funds from Tony Tenser's Tigon Films and ambitious independent Pat Curtis's Curtwel. Tigon, which evolved out of Compton Cameo, were an exploitation outfit, typically turning out the likes of Vernon Sewell's *The Blood Beast Terror* (1967) and Gerry O'Hara's *The Body Stealers* (1969), but Tenser and sometime partner Michael Klinger had backed Roman Polanski on *Repulsion* (1965) and *Cul-de-Sac* (1966). A one-time child actor (Scarlett O'Hara's baby in *Gone With the Wind*, 1939), Curtis had grown up to become the manager, husband and promoter of Raquel Welch (hence the name of their jointly-owned company). Reports of the budget vary from 'about £52,000' (David Pirie) to '£25,000, out of which Karloff would take £11,000' (Iain Sinclair).

Sinclair, who knocked about with Reeves and Baker and worked on intriguing unmade projects ranging from a science fiction musical vehicle for The Shadows to an early draft of what became *Conan the Barbarian* (1982), reports 'Reeves wasn't short of bottle. He flew straight out to Spain, hoping to snare Boris Karloff. The veteran horror star, ex-Uppingham School, was happy to chat to another public school fellow – even if the bounder didn't have much interest in cricket. Anything would be an improvement on recent labours, such as *The Ghost in the Invisible Bikini*' (1966). Karloff fans and scholars have rather overlooked *The Sorcerers*, overshadowed as it is at the very end of the star's career by the semi-biographical *Targets* (1968). *Midnight Marquee Actors Series: Boris Karloff*, a collection of essays edited by Gary J. and Susan Svehla, includes affectionate and detailed accounts of *Charlie Chan at the Opera* (1937) and *Die, Monster, Die!* (1965) but nothing on *The Sorcerers*. However, Sinclair reports that Karloff was interested enough in the project to insist 'upon revisions to the script, which not only made him, in some senses, a co-author, bit also the man responsible for bringing an unlooked for dignity and depth to the proceedings. The one-dimensional notion of an evil genius (yet another crazed scientist) getting his rocks off by plugging into the under-financed dregs of swinging London was unacceptable to Karloff. He wasn't prepared to walk through it and pick up the cheque.

There was enough gravitas in his hardwon screen persona to inspire the novice director—who was happy to make adjustments to the outline.' At the Science Fiction Film Festival in Trieste, Karloff and co-star Catherine Lacey took the Best Actor and Actress prizes.

Ian Ogilvy is as usual cast as a hero who is clearly the director's stand-in (his character name is 'Mike Roscoe'), uppercrust enough to have a good address but trying to put on a rough, classless voice, spending his days in a customer-free junk/antiques shop called The Glory Hole, and his nights at a tiny, crowded disco called Blazes. Sinclair suggests 'the restlessness, the non-job, the apparent means to do whatever he wants to do, is a sympathetic caricature of Reeves' own dilemma—Ogilvy is a smoother Reeves with terminal angst, other-directed, given to contact the violent, risk-taking aspects of himself.' Given the jumble of genres, as gothic horror and mind-bending science fiction collide with hallucinogenic teen flick and London lout movie, it's still jarring to find a scene in which Karloff, white-bearded and dark-skinned, limps into a Wimpy Bar to pick up 'pill-popper' Ogilvy over a burger, promising 'ecstasy without consequence'. It is also striking that the chintzy, faded, cluttered home Karloff's 'medical hypnotist' Professor Marcus Monserrat makes with his harridan wife Estelle (Lacey) contains a blinding white *Alphaville* room full of science fiction apparatus and trippy brainwashing effects out of *The Ipcress File* (1965) or *A Clockwork Orange* (1971).

Karloff, who certainly was capable of walking through and picking up the cheque, relishes not only the chance to have scenes worth playing but the challenge of acting opposite someone who can hold her own with him. Lacey, a veteran of everything from *The Lady Vanishes* (1938) and *Whisky Galore* (1949) then fresh from a ham turn as a mad prophetess in Hammer's *The Mummy's Shroud* (1967), is extraordinary as the film's witchlike villainness. Decades of genteel poverty and unspoken desires have ground Estelle down, but she blossoming nastily as she first uses Mike to replace her ratty fur-collared cloth coat with something white and endangered then indulges in random excitement—a midnight swim in a private pool in Dolphin Square, a ton-up jaunt on a 'borrowed' motorbike —and eventually ultra-violence. The sex is implicit, in the mini-dressed forms of Elizabeth Ercy, Susan George and Dani Sheridan; the violence comes in quick flashes, as Mike reaches for the scissors to gut George or throttles a 'slag' in an alleyway. *The Sorcerers* isn't as extravagantly gory as *Witchfinder General*, but its fight scenes are credibly ugly, inept scuffles in a garage or the antiques shop, with Mike and his tagalong mate Alan (Victor Henry) clinching and pummelling, doing a lot of damage to their surroundings but not each other. It's a despairing vision, of generations not so much in conflict as collaboration, soullessly feeding each other's worst instincts.

The most recognisable face in the supporting cast is Susan George, a year or so away from starletdom, but for the money, the film gets some useful minor acting talent. Victor Henry, luckless third wheel here, had been in Peter Watkins's *Privilege* and would be in George's breakthrough vehicle *All Neat in Black Stockings* (1968); his career then ended when he was left comatose after being knocked down by a speeding car (he died in 1985). Familiar face Ivor Dean plays the trenchcoated police inspector with a Maigret pipe and hat, as he had done on the TV series *The Saint*; his genre credits include *Theatre of Death* (1967), *The Oblong Box* (1969, which would have been Reeves's post-*Witchfinder* film) and bodysnatcher William Burke in *Dr Jekyll and Sister Hyde* (1971). Elizabeth (sometimes Elisabeth) Ercy had been French dressing in *Doctor in Clover* (1966) but was probably seen by Pat Curtis alongside Raquel Welch in *Fathom* (1967), while Dani Sheridan's only other significant credit is as a minor Bond girl in *On Her Majesty's Secret Service* (1971). Alf Joint, who plays Alan's mechanic boss, was a stuntman (later stunt co-ordinator) on big budget shot-in-Britain productions like the *Superman* films. Martin Terry, the newsagent, was a Reeves regular, with roles in *Witchfinder* and *The Oblong Box*. And Gerald Campion, who has a one-scene turn as a nasty gay customer in Mike's china shop, was famous in the 1950s as Billy Bunter on British television; a busy bit-player, he was also the proprietor of Gerry's Club in Soho.

On the technical side, Reeves employs a rogue's gallery of British fringe cinema worthies. Art director Tony (not the famous one) Curtis would later work regularly for Amicus Films (*Tales From the Crypt*, 1972) and marry Hammer starlet Yutte Stensgaard. Cinematographer Stanley A. Long was a long-serving exploitation fixture who directed the likes of *On the Game* (1975) and *Adventures of a Plumber's Mate* (1978) but made his fortune as a distributor with that staple of early video rental shops Alpha Films. Credited as 'executive producer' is Long's frequent partner Arnold Louis Miller, the man behind *Nudes of the World* (1961) and *Take Off Your Clothes and Live* (1962) and also the driving force of Global-Queensway Pictures, specialists in the agonisingly dull travelogue shorts that cluttered up 'full supporting programs' for most of the 1970s (until the genre was killed off by the spoof, *Getting Away From It All*, 1979). As with *Witchfinder*, the music comes from Paul Ferris, who is in jazzier mood here, providing the nightclub songs 'Your Love' and 'Sweet Nothing' as performed by Toni Daly (dubbing Sheridan) and The Capitols – though there's a presumably unauthorised snatch of Cliff Richards singing 'Out in the Country' on a Dansette record-player. Ferris's all-too-few post-Reeves credits include *The Creeping Flesh* (1973), *Persecution* (1974) and *Harry and the Hookers* (1976). Make-up artist Geoff Rodway, whose major challenge comes in the very last scene, had created the feathery freak for *The Vulture* (1966) but was kept busiest as a mainstay of the long-running *Carry On* saga. Though the credited editors are David Woodward and Susan Michie, the work was mostly done by Ralph Sheldon who worked with Seth Holt on *Never Let Go* (1960) and has credits on films from *Night of the Eagle* (1963) through *The Likely Lads* (1976) to *Shanghai Surprise* (1986).

The Sorcerers was respectably reviewed for its genre, with none of the vehement controversy that erupted around *Matthew Hopkins, Witchfinder General*. In Variety, 'Rich' noted 'a straightforward thriller slanted to "horror" addicts . . . Reeves, a young director who also co-scripted the yarn, has done a commendable job . . . Karloff handles his role with notable professionalism.' The anonymous reviewer of the *Monthly Film Bulletin* wins points for spotting Reeves's talent early, though felt the film a retrograde step after *Revenge of the Blood Beast*. The *MFB* tags 'a script which comes as close to authentic *Sadisme* as anything since *Peeping Tom* . . . it is the overall effect that impresses rather than any individual scene or composition, but the "psychedelic experience" is particularly well done, with the victim's face literally disintegrating in blobs of colour'. For David Pirie, who admires the movie, 'the film stops short of being a masterpiece', but Iain Sinclair, in much the best piece of writing on *The Sorcerers*, declares it 'thematically, the more complex and interesting of the two major Reeves features . . . resolutely stopped down, locked in the skull, an unacknowledged and genuine contribution to London's covert filmography.'

MICHAEL REEVES – BRITAIN'S LOST HORROR PRODIGY

Tony Earnshaw

WHEN MICHAEL REEVES DIED, AGED JUST 24, IN 1969 FROM an accidental overdose of barbiturates, one of Britain's most brilliant filmmaking talents died with him. In a career lasting just five years, Reeves had gained a reputation for highly stylised and unique film-making on the basis of just four-and-a-half movies. They included *Castle of the Living Dead, Revenge of the Blood Beast, The Sorcerers*, the seminal shocker *Matthew Hopkins Witchfinder General* and *The Oblong Box*, on which Reeves had just begun working when he died in his sleep. In the 42 years since he died, Reeves has been largely forgotten within global horror circles, eclipsed by directors like Terence Fisher, Freddie Francis and, perhaps, John Gilling, who churned out dozens of low-budget chillers in long and sometimes turbulent careers.

Yet Reeves' films, particularly the grim and unrelenting *Matthew Hopkins Witchfinder General* (known in the States as *The Conqueror Worm*), have kept his name alive among British fans, who recognise the touch of genius in the film which unquestionably contains Vincent Price's career-best performance. In a century of filmmaking Britain has produced only a handful of horror pictures which can be rightly described as classics. Among them are *Dead of Night, Night of the Demon, Night of the Eagle, The Innocents*, Hammer's *The Curse of Frankenstein, Dracula* and *The Brides of Dracula*, and Robin Hardy's *The Wicker Man. Matthew Hopkins Witchfinder General* is up there with the best of them—a terri-fying, brutal tale, based on truth and boasting all the best that sheer horror and Grand Guignol can offer.

Born in 1944, Reeves, a cineaste and film scholar, broke into movies by flying to Los Angeles and brazenly turning up on the doorstep of his idol, the American director Don Siegel, to ask for a job. Siegel, himself a film fan as well as a filmmaker, took him on as a dialogue director. Returning to England, Reeves graduated a few rungs up the ladder, working as a gofer on movies like *The Long Ships* and *Genghis Khan* before moving into television commercials. Another break came via producer Paul Maslansky, who allowed Reeves to work on a few scripts and engaged him as assistant director on *Castle of the Living Dead*, a cheapie European horror being shot in Italy starring Christopher Lee.

When director Warren Kiefer became sick, Reeves was encouraged to bump up his contribution and with a second unit shot some stylish footage, including a circus sequence featuring Donald Sutherland as a witch.

Reeves' work resulted in Maslansky offering him a script, Vardella, which was to be variously re-titled *Revenge of the Blood Beast, Satan's Sister* and *The She-Beast*. Italian favourite Barbara Steele starred as an indestructible witch. Though it was shot on a minuscule budget, and the script (re-written by Reeves under a nom-de-plume) was somewhat tedious, *Revenge of the Blood Beast* illustrated the promise of what Reeves could do with a banal horror movie.

Back in England after his Italian sojourn, Reeves battled to set up new projects and eventually, with friend and partner Tom Baker, rewrote a script from John Burke's original screenplay *The Sorcerers*. The eventual movie, again shot on a tiny budget, would star horror legend Boris Karloff and Catherine Lacey as an elderly married couple who, through a unique method of hypnosis, can live vicariously through young people and feel their emotions. An intense combination of horror movie and *Peeping Tom* style voyeurism, it provided yet more building blocks for the reputation Reeves was beginning to forge—that of an original and highly inventive young filmmaker. Reeves' brief but brilliant career reached its peak with *Matthew Hopkins Witchfinder General* in 1968, a project he had adapted, with Tom Baker, from the dry historical novel by Ronald Bassett.

The project was picked up by American International Pictures, which hired Reeves to direct his own script but disagreed with him over his choice of star. Reeves wanted Donald Pleasence; he got Vincent Price. From day one Reeves and Price were at loggerheads, principally because Reeves openly revealed he was unhappy with the casting of Price. He felt the 56-year-old star was too identified with the OTT films of Roger Corman, and that his acting was hammy and affected. Over the five-week shoot the Young Turk and the old star frequently locked horns. Reeves told Price not to shake his head, to play down his character, the witchfinder Matthew Hopkins, and present him as a menacing psychotic. Price, shaken at his director's obvious dislike of him, concentrated on the job and in doing so gave the performance of his career. Hopkins emerges as cold, reptilian, dead-eyed, mercenary and murderous.

In a stark film he is the starkest thing in it - a sinister figure in black scything through the English countryside plucking innocents at random and hanging or burning them as witches until he is brought down by the power of good, represented by a young soldier. *Matthew Hopkins Witchfinder General* was a big success for AIP, and for Reeves, who succeeded, almost single-handedly, in changing the face of the British horror film. Despite their differences, Reeves and Price were scheduled to work together again on two other pictures: *The Oblong Box* and *Scream and Scream Again*. Both men got as far as costume fittings and preparation for the first when Reeves was found dead. (Both films would eventually be made by Gordon Hessler).

An inquest recorded an open verdict, but Reeves had apparently over-dosed on barbiturates. Producer Tony Tenser claims his death was accidental, that Reeves went to bed with a headache, took some tablets, still had the headache and took some more. Independently wealthy and with "a nice girlfriend", Reeves, said Tenser, would never have killed himself.

Price had a different opinion. He claimed Reeves was unstable and had attempted suicide frequently before; having broken up with his girlfriend, he finally succeeded. And so as Reeves died, a myth was born. Forty years and more later, he remains a lost talent—a young man on the verge of massive success who, like James Dean, died before he could truly realise his tremendous gifts.

Michael Reeves
Born: October 17, 1944
Died: February 11, 1969

Michael Reeves Filmography

1959 *Intrusion* (student short) (dir)
1960 *Carrion* (student short) (dir)
1960 *Flaming Star* (observer)
1963 *The Long Ships* (dialogue coach)
1964 *Genghis Khan* (runner)
1965 *Castle of the Living Dead* (2nd unit dir, co-scr, both uncredited)
1966 *Revenge of the Blood Beast* (dir, co-scr)
1967 *The Sorcerers* (dir, prod, co-scr)
1968 *Witchfinder General* (dir, co-scr)
1968 *The Oblong Box* (pre-prod work as dir)

Screen Files © Tony Earnshaw/Reel Solutions 1999/2011

John Burke's Letters

ROOPER & WHATELY.

G.A. WHATELY.
S.E. THOMPSON.
R.D. POWELL.
H.D. GRUNDY.

E.G. WHATELY.

TELEPHONE HOLBORN. 7077
7078
7079
INLAND TELEGRAMS BIENNIALLY,
FOREIGN CABLES: LONDON,
W.C.2.

17. LINCOLN'S INN FIELDS.

LONDON, W.C.2.

7th July, 1966.

16/CR.

Dear Mr. Burke,

<u>Leith Productions Limited</u>,

Thank you for your letter of the 6th July. I am
sorry that you should confuse a misunderstanding with bad faith.
I have however now spoken to Mr. Reeves and he has cleared up
the misunderstanding, and I confirm that terms as set out in
your letter are correct. I have today sent a cheque for £250
in your favour to your agents and will send a Contract in the
course of a few days although I feel the whole matter is more
than covered by the correspondence.

J. Burke, Esq.,
31 Garden Royal,
Kersfield Road,
London. S.W.15.

Yours sincerely

CURTWEL PRODUCTIONS Inc.

9777 Wilshire Blvd. Suite 800
Beverly Hills, California, 90212

CRestview 8-1500
TRemont 8-2500
Cable Address : Litlaw

PATRICK CURTIS - *President*
RAQUEL WELCH - *Vice-President*
BARRY HIRSCH - *Sec. Treasurer*

15 Grosvenor Crescent Mews
London, SW1   England

BELgravia 6326

August 18, 1966

Mr. John Burke,

    Dear Mr. Burke, this letter and the enclosed check for £55 will
constitute an agreement between us the screen option to "The Devil's
Discord" for a period of six (6) months. The aforementioned £55 is the
agreed 10% of the full purchase price of the treatment which will be
£550. The remainder to be paid not later than six months from the above
date. If the option is picked up.

    It is understood that the rights assigned to us are exclusive to us
for the above said time.

Yours Sincerely,

Patrick Curtis

24th August 1966

Patrick Curtis Esq
Curtwel Productions Inc

Dear Mr Curtis,

Many thanks for your letter of 18th August and the cheque for £55.

I confirm that this constitutes an agreement between us for my screen treatment, THE DEVIL'S DISCORD, the £55 being a 10% advance on the full purchase price of £550 of which the remainder shall be paid not later than 18th February 1967 if you decide to pick up this option.

During this period I will not offer the material elsewhere.

Yours sincerely,

24th August 1966

Dear Mike,

The cheque and letter have arrived safely. Many thanks.

You did say on the phone that you would also be enclosing Patrick Curtis's present address in Rome so that I could send a confirmatory letter direct to him. It wasn't enclosed, however, so I think the safest thing is for me to leave the addressing of the enclosed envelope to you. I'd be grateful if you would send it on.

Hope all your projects are flourishing.

All the best,

CURTWEL PRODUCTIONS Inc.

9777 Wilshire Blvd. Suite 800
Beverly Hills, California, 90212

CRestview 8-1500
TRemont 8-2500
Cable Address : Litlaw

PATRICK CURTIS - *President*
RAQUEL WELCH - *Vice-President*
BARRY HIRSCH - *Sec. Treasurer*

15 Grosvenor Crescent Mews
London, SW1   England

BELgravia 6326

Sept. 18, 1966

Mr. John Burke,

This will confirm our verbal agreement of last week concerning the
script of "Devil's Discord". You will deliver to us as sole owners the
aforementioned screenplay under the following conditions:

1. 10% option on treatment ——————————— £55 (paid)
2. Option pickup ——————————— £495
3. Upon commencement of screenplay ——————— £500
4. Upon completion of screenplay ————————— £250
5. On first day of shooting ————————— £500
                                        ————
                        TOTAL   £1,800

It is understood that the completed screenplay will contain all
necessary rewrites, revisions and additions as agreed upon by the producer.

Sincerely,

Patrick Curtis

20th September 1966

Mike Reeves Esq
23 Yeomans Row
London S.W.3

Dear Mike,

Herewith two pages of notes on THE DEVIL'S DISCORD.
I hope they're what you need - and so far as I'm concerned,
I think they'll add more than enough to bring the picture
up to length.   I've enclosed a carbon in case you want to
pass one copy on and retain one.

I do hope we can get agreement to the idea of
Barbarina being the caretaker's wife rather than his
daughter.   A sign of my faith in this idea is that I go
on believing in spite of the fact that it will mean a lot
more rewriting and retyping for me!

If you can let me know about progress by Wednesday
morning before I go to Liverpool, so much the better.   In
any case I think the next stage is to get everyone's views
on what the final screenplay should be, so that I can go
ahead with it and not have to play about with it again
because someone has forgotten to shove his oar in.   This
rushing and skimping never produces good work.   My own
feeling now is that, once I've got final details and the
go-ahead from you, I should produce a watertight shooting
script for delivery to you by Monday 3rd October.   If you
want it sooner than that, it will be just another rushed
job.

The present first draft is, I think, adequate for
casting and costing, taking into account the additional
notes.

Let me know the worst, anyway.

Yours,

5th October 1966

G. A. Whately Esq
Messrs Rooper & Whately
17 Lincoln's Inn Fields
London W.C.2

Dear Mr Whateley,

THE DEVIL'S DISCORD

   Further to our telephone conversation this afternoon,
I enclose a copy of Patrick Curtis's letter to me of 18th
September. I think this makes the terms of our agreement
clear. I would add that for quite some time before this
letter was finally extracted from Mr Curtis I had been asking
for a contract to be drawn up, and when the letter was given
to me I was assured that it was merely the preliminary to a
contract which was in course of preparation. Taking the
word of the gentlemen concerned, I wrote a first draft
screenplay and then went on to a completely revised final
screenplay. So far I have received only the £55 option
payment. What is now due to me is:

Option pickup	£495
Commencement of screenplay.	£500
Completion of screenplay...	£250
	£ 1,245

   I realise that you were not given these details until
very recently, but I hope that with the information now
available you will be able to arrange payment of this sum
not later than Friday, 14th October 1966. If a cheque
for the amount due is not forthcoming by then, I'm afraid
that in order to protect my own interests I shall have to
take legal proceedings - which I'm most reluctant to do, I
assure you.

          Yours sincerely,

CURTWEL PRODUCTIONS Inc.

9777 Wilshire Blvd. Suite 800
Beverly Hills, California, 90212

CRestview 8-1500
TRemont 8-2500
Cable Address : Lidlaw

PATRICK CURTIS - *President*
RAQUEL WELCH - *Vice-President*
BARRY HIRSCH - *Sec. Treasurer*

15 Grosvenor Crescent Mews
London, SW1   England

BELgravia 6326

10 · 10 · 66.

John Burke
31, Garden Royal,
Kensfield Road.
S.W. 15.

Dear Mr. Burke,

Enclosed is a cheque for £595 which Mr. Whately asked to be paid by Mr. Curtis for the script of "Devils Discord". The rest of the money will come from Mr. Whately on behalf of Mr. Reeves.

I trust that all will then be in order; and apologise for the delays which have occurred.

Yours sincerely

Bridget A. Swan.

THE SORCERERS

ROOPER & WHATELY.

G. A. WHATELY.
R. E. THOMPSON.
R. G. POWELL.
H. D. GRUNDY.

E. G. WHATELY.

TELEPHONE:- HOLBORN. 7077.
7078.
7079.
INLAND TELEGRAMS (BIENNIALLY,
FOREIGN CABLES:- { LONDON.
W.C.2.

17. LINCOLN'S INN FIELDS.

LONDON, W.C.2.

16/SH

1st December, 1966.

Dear Mr. Burke,

Re: 'TERROR FOR KICKS'

      I understand from Mr. Reeves that you do not
wish to carry out any further rewriting of this script
and that in view of this, you would be prepared to
forego your right to the sum of £750. payable on the
first day of principal photography.

      If you would please confirm that these terms
are agreed, I will prepare a simple Agreement for
signature and presumably you would wish this to be dealt
with through Mrs. Robin Dalton.

               Yours sincerely,

J. Burke, Esq.,
31, Garden Royal,
Kersfield Road,
S.W.15.

2nd December 1966

Mrs Robin Dalton
Theatrework(London) Ltd
22 Hans Road
London S.W.3

Dear Robin,

I hope you will by now be back from the States and able to tidy up a point regarding TERROR FOR KICKS.

You may remember that when you went away the Mike Reeves and Pat Curtis partnership had shelved TERROR FOR KICKS and were about to embark on THE DEVIL'S DISCORD. I went off to Broadstairs – and when I got back it was to learn that there had been casting trouble, Compton had backed out, and THE DEVIL'S DISCORD could not yet be made. But Boris Karloff would appear in TERROR FOR KICKS if a rewrite was done to build up his part and alter the story somewhat. Mike Reeves wanted to know if I could drop everything and rewrite it to Karloff's wishes in a week or so.

I had really had about enough of these folk, and after thinking it over I rang back and said I was too busy on another project (which is true) and couldn't do further work. My agreement on TERROR FOR KICKS had been fulfilled, I had done rewrites for which I was asked, and had been paid off – save for £750 due on first day of principal photography. As they were in a spot I offered to let them have this £750 for any other writer they got to work on the project.

I have now had the enclosed letter from Rooper and Whately. A darned sight quicker off the mark than they were when they owed me money! I also enclose a carbon of my acknowledgment of the letter. I'd be glad if you would sort this out speedily. My own feeling is that if they have to pay the full £750 for a full rewrite, I'll waive all further claim on it – though legally, of course, I'm really still entitled to the lot whatever they may do – but that if they don't need too much rewriting, and in fact do it themselves or get it done for, say, £250, the balance of the £750 ought still to be payable to me. You, as my agent, can be tougher with R&W on this score than I would be.

Love,

2nd December 1966

G. A. Whately Esq
Messrs Hooper & Whately
17 Lincoln's Inn Fields
London W.C.2

Dear Mr Whately,

TERROR FOR KICKS

Thank you for your letter of 1st December, a copy of
which I am sending to Mrs Robin Dalton so that she can
take up the details of an Agreement with you.

As you will realise, I fulfilled all the terms of my
original contract for this title and could in no way be
considered under an obligation to do further rewriting.
I would therefore, also, be entitled to the full £750 on
first day of principal photography. My offer to waive
this payment was made simply to help Mr Reeves out of a
difficulty, even though this difficulty was no
responsibility of mine.

In the circumstances I think that it should be
clearly established that I forego my right to the sum of
£750 on the understanding that this sum is to be spent on
another author's work on the script.   If it happened,
for instance, that the project were suspended for a while
and then it was decided to go ahead, after all, with my
original script on which no further money had been spent,
I would naturally not wish to have signed away the £750.
Similarly, if only a certain amount of editorial work is
required and it turns out that this costs only £250 or
so, then I think the balance of the £750 should come to
me.

In all events it should be understood that I still
expect a major screen credit for my share of the script
and also for the original story from which it was
developed.

Perhaps you and Mrs Dalton will sort out the details
between you.

Yours sincerely,

-559-

ROOPER & WHATELY.

G. A. WHATELY.
R. E. THOMPSON.
R. O. POWELL.
H. O. GRUNDY.

E. G. WHATELY.

TELEPHONE:- HOLBORN. 7077.
7078.
7079.
INLAND TELEGRAMS. } BIENNIALLY,
FOREIGN CABLES:- } LONDON,
W.C.2.

17, LINCOLN'S INN FIELDS.

LONDON, W.C.2.

16/SH

14th December, 1966.

Dear Mr. Burke,

Thank you for your letter of the 2nd December.
I understand that there will be no objection to the terms
which you quoted in your letter and I will accordingly
prepare a short Agreement for signature.

Yours sincerely,

J. Burke, Esq.,
31, Garden Royal,
Kersfield Road,
S.W.15.

ROBIN DALTON ASSOCIATES

THEATREWORK (LONDON) LIMITED

22, Hans Road, London S.W.3   KNI 3262
Directors Elspeth Cochrane, Warren Tute & David White

Cables TEEWORK LONDON

30th December, 1966

John Burke Esq.,
31 Garden Royal,
Kersfield Road,
S.W.15.

Dear John,

I finally have a draft agreement for you from
Hooper & Whately which seems to me to be
perfectly in order.

It seems a terrible waste of time that they
should have to send us a draft, and I am
telling them by the same post, to go ahead
and draw up a fair copy but you may like to
see the draft nevertheless.

Yours ever,

Robin Dalton

2nd January 1967

Mrs Robin Dalton
Theatrework (London) Ltd
22 Hans Road
London S.W.3

Dear Robin,

I suppose the draft agreement from Rooper & Whately
is in order, though frankly I'm not too happy about the
wording of para 2.

If you look at my original letters to you and to
Whately on the subject, you'll see that I particularly
wanted to cover the question of Leith Productions paying
out, perhaps, only a small proportion of the £750 and
my then, as it were, handing back to them money which ought
still to come to me on first day of shooting. I know
that in para 1 the phrasing is that I will forego from the
£750 "such sum as Leith shall expend on the rewriting ...
etc" and this might seem to cover the matter; but by
adding in para 2 that they shall have full discretion to
employ anyone they choose and pay what they choose, aren't
they making it all too easy to dodge? I mean, if they do
three sentences of rewriting on two or three pages and
decide to pay Michael Reeves himself £750 for this arduous
task, what redress would I have?

I had hoped this was something you'd be able to avoid
in some way or other. If you can't see any simple way of
doing it, however, I suppose we'll have to wear it.

Do joggle the memories of your friends in New York
about THE TWISTED TONGUES from time to time, won't you?

Love,

Further Reading

F OR THE SEMI-OFFICIAL VERSION OF TIGON, SEE HAMILTON, J. (2005), *Beasts in the Cellar: The Exploitation Film Career of Tony Tenser*, London: FAB Press. For the history of AIP, see McGee, M. T. (2011), *Faster and Furiouser: The Revised and Fattened Fable of American International Pictures*, North Carolina: McFarland and Co., Inc. See Curti, R. (2011), *Fantasmi d'amore. Il gotico italiano tra cinema, letteratura e tv*, Turin: Lindau.

Movie sought to specialise in the serious discussion of genre film-making over *Sight and Sound's* then propensity for art house cinema, and so Reeves would have been, Wood notes, the ideal subject for extended consideration. See Wood, R. 'In memoriam Michael Reeves', Movie (Winter 1969-70). Reproduced at:

www2.warwick.ac.uk/fac/arts/film/movie/contents/in_memorium_michael_reeves.pdf

Also, Halligan, B. (2003), *Michael Reeves*, Manchester: Manchester University Press. For more on Reeves, see: Cranfield, I. (2007), *At Last Michael Reeves: An Investigative Memoir of the Acclaimed Filmmaker*, Lulu.com; Murray, J. B. (2002, revised 2004), *The Remarkable Michael Reeves: His Short and Tragic Life*, Baltimore: Midnight Marquee Press; Sinclair, I. (1997), *Lights Out for the Territory: 9 Excursions into the Secret History of London*, London: Granta. Pirie, D. (1973), *A Heritage of Horror: The English Gothic Cinema* 1946-1972, London: Gordon Fraser. The book was updated and republished in 2008 as *A New Heritage of Horror: The English Gothic Cinema*, London: I. B. Tauris. Hardy, P. (1986), *Horror* (Aurum Film Encyclopedia), London: Hamlyn. Paul Maslansky; interview with the author, 27 November 2011.

About the Author

JOHN FREDERICK BURKE WAS BORN IN RYE, SUSSEX ON March 8, 1922, and educated at Holt High School, Liverpool. He served in the Royal Air Force, Royal Electrical and Mechanical Engineers, and the Royal Marines during the war.

After working for the publishers Museum Press and the Books for Pleasure Group, he was a Public Relations and Publications Executive for Shell (1959–63) and Story Editor for Twentieth Century-Fox (1963–65) before becoming a full-time writer in 1966. Writing as Jonathan Burke, J.F. Burke and John Burke, he produced several suspense stories and psychological thrillers, including the Atlantic Award in Literature winning *Swift Summer* (1949; by J.F. Burke), *These Haunted Streets* (1950), *Chastity House* (1952), *Echo of Barbara* (1959; filmed in 1960) and *The Twisted Tongues* (1964). Some of his other novels appeared under the pseudonyms of Joanna Jones, Sara Morris, Jonathan George and Owen Burke.

He achieved equal popularity with his science fiction short stories in magazines like *New Worlds* and *New Frontiers*, and the best of these were collected in *Alien Landscapes* (1955). His first two SF novels, *The Dark Gateway* (1953) and *The Echoing World* (1954), both dealt with the theme of parallel universes; and *Pursuit Through Time* (1956) described an attempt to change the course of history while time-travelling into the past.

For over thirty years John Burke novelised a large number of stage plays, film and TV scripts, notably John Osborne's *The Entertainer* (1960) and *Look Back in Anger* (1960), *The Angry Silence* (1960), *Flame in the Streets* (1961), *The Lion of Sparta* (1961; the film was released as *The 300 Spartans*), *The Boys* (1962), *The System* (1963), *A Hard Day's Night* (1964), *Dr. Terror's House of Horrors* (1965), *That Magnificent Air Race*

(1965; the film was released as *Those Magnificent Men in Their Flying Machines*), *The Hammer Horror Omnibus* (1966/7; two volumes), *Till Death Us Do Part* (1967), *Privilege* (1967), *Smashing Time* (1968), Ian Fleming's *Chitty Chitty Bang Bang* (1968), *Moon Zero Two* (1969), *Luke's Kingdom* (1976), *King and Castle* (1986) and a series of *The Bill* novels, beginning in 1985.

Several other tie-ins appeared under the names of Martin Sands and Robert Miall, including *Maroc 7* (1967), *The Best House in London* (1969), two *Jason King* thrillers in 1972 and also *UFO* and its sequel *UFO 2* (1970/1971).

He also wrote the source story and the original screenplay for the 1967 cult horror film *The Sorcerers* and contributed to the TV series *Late Night Horror* (BBC 1968), *Tales of Unease* (LWT 1970) and *The Frighteners* (LWT 1972).

Among John Burke's later novels were a series featuring the Victorian psychic investigator and occult detective Dr Alex Caspian (a stage magician by day, assisted by his wife, Bronwen), and a further three Victorian Gothic suspense novels (by 'Harriet Esmond') written in collaboration with his wife Jean. They were always carefully researched and explored the regions described in these stories.

He edited a trilogy of books under the 'Unease' banner, *Tales of Unease* (1966), *More Tales of Unease* (1969) and *New Tales of Unease* (1976). Several ghost and horror stories appeared in the Pan 'Ghost Book' series, the infamous *Pan Book of Horror Stories*, *New Terrors*, *The Mammoth Book of Best New Horror* and his short stories were collected in the Ash Tree Press volume *We've Been Waiting For You* (2000), which included his most celebrated story, *And Cannot Come Again*.

He wrote two original short stories that were published in *Back From The Dead: The Legacy of the Pan Book of Horror Stories* (2010). Robert Hale also published five novels in the last decade; *Stalking Widow* (2000), *The Second Strain* (2002), *Wrong Turnings* (2004), *Hang Time* (2007) and *The Merciless Dead* (2008). His posthumous horror novel, *The Nightmare Whisperers* (2012) was started in the 50s, filed away and resurfaced when John told Johnny Mains about its existence and Mains urged him to finish it.

Burke also wrote over twenty non-fiction titles including several travel books for Batsford: *Suffolk* (1971), *Sussex* (1974), *English Villages* (1975), *Czechoslovakia* (1976) and *The English Inn* (1981).

John died in September 2011 and survived by his wife Jean (née Williams) and their two sons David and Edmund, and also by five daughters; Bronwen, Jennie, Sally, Joan and Jane from his first marriage to Joan (née Morris).

JOHNNY MAINS WAS BORN IN GALASHIELS, ROXBURGHSHIRE, on 15 April 1976, and educated at Earlston High School. He is the British Fantasy Award winning editor of *Back From The Dead: The Legacy of the Pan Book of Horror Stories* (2010). He has also edited *Bite Sized Horror* (2011), *The Screaming Book of Horror* (2012) and *The Burning Circus* (2013). Mains has also written the official biography of Herbert van Thal, *Lest You Should Suffer Nightmares*, which was nominated for a British Fantasy Award for Best Non-Fiction. Mains is also an author of horror fiction, his two collections are *With Deepest Sympathy* (2010) and *Frightfully Cosy and Mild Stories For Nervous Types* (2012).

INT.   RECORD SHOP   EARLY EVENING

3

. In a hooded booth a
c is that of the club,
ak.

29

7

10 Continued

to the music. PENNY is a girl of wide gestures,
always on the go, spreading her arms, grimacing,
bobbing her head - but she must not be just an
affected, irritating show-off.
infectious, even if Mike doesn't

SINGER or BAND number finishes C
APPLAUSE O.S.

                    PENNY
        Oh, do stop fiddling and
        back.   (holds out hand

MIKE stares at her and delibera
out to its full length, holding
throat as though to slit it.

                    MIKE
        Better to end it all no

                    PENNY
        Mike ... don't fool ar
        quite sharp.

MIKE makes her wait. Then he
fraction of an inch away from
whizz shut. PENNY opens her
tosses the spool accurately in

                    MIKE
        Didn't you want to see
        real blood in my veins

                    PENNY
        I'll bet it's just ac
        would corrode my tape

                    MIKE

8

16   Continued

                    MIKE
        You know what a sensualis
        I get an added frisson fr
        presence of your jealous a

                    PENNY
        For all the frissons I've
        you get, you might as well
        a ... well, a Martian.

                    MIKE
        A Martian ... You know, th
        explain a lot.

PENNY stands up and waves to Alan O.S
back musing.

                    MIKE
        I've always felt I was an alie
        this odd world. Sent here on
        strange mission. I wonder ...

ALAN COMES INTO SHOP.

                    ALAN
        Hello, Mike. Penny. Sorry I'
        late.

                    MIKE
        The terrestrial time scale means
        nothing to us Martians.

ALAN is clearly used to this kind of thing
amiably at PENNY and looks round for a spac

                    PENNY
        I suppose no-one's going to be forw
        enough to ask me to dance?

                    ALAN
        I'm good at the gavotte, and better
        at the bourrée.
                (puts out his hand
                 to her)
        Shall we -

                    MIKE
                (getting up)
        Let's move on.

9

10

59 Continued

                    ALAN
        If you've got to be told, you're
        not with us, you ain't got it.

                    PENNY
        Tell me all the same.

        ...wards the door. As they approach it,
        ...doorway. He looks thoughtful,
        ...draws ALAN's attention
        ...r. They are

159 Continued   73

                    PENNY
        He must be ... out buying something.
        New stock. Or something.

        I hope so.   ALAN

                    PENNY
        He ... he'd hardly met her before
        last night, had he?

                    ALAN
        How should I know? I'm beginning
        to wonder if we've ever really
        known anything about him.

PENNY tries pressing the bell, jabbing
time to ...
                   clamorous al...

6   69

154 INT.   MESMER'S ROOM - CU ESTELLE   NIGHT

ESTELLE is gloating, staring straight at us, urging
the whole thing on.
                                        CUT TO:

155 EXT.   TWO SHOT MIKE AND LAURA IN LANE   NIGHT

Very close on the two of them. MIKE strangling
LAURA. She is hardly stirring now.

                    MIKE
        Why won't you sing when I ask
        you? You'll never take it -
        never be a star. Never ...   CAM MOVES IN

LAURA moans once and then is still.   the eyes
on MIKE's face. It is blank and cruel,
quite dead.   Then he blinks and shakes his head.
Twists his head towards us so that he is in full CU.
Puts one hand shakily to his forehead.
                                        CUT TO:

156 INT.   MESMER'S ROOM - CU MESMER   NIGHT

MESMER, staring straight ahead, begins to shake.
He looks alarmed.

                    MESMER
        He's drifting away from us.

                    ESTELLE (O.S.)
        I can't feel ... can't se ...

CAM PULLS BACK to take in ESTELLE and MESMER.

                    MESMER
        The drug has weakened.

                    MESMER
        We ought never to have risked it.

                    ESTELLE
                (moaning)
        He's going ...

                    MESMER
        Hold him - we must hold him!
                                        CUT TO:

for so long that
plays abstractedly with
He draws it out, snaps i   ...hes at a time
by stabbing the button.